JUDAS AND THE
GOSPEL OF JESUS

JUDAS AND THE
GOSPEL OF JESUS

Have We Missed the Truth about Christianity?

N. T. WRIGHT

BakerBooks
Grand Rapids, Michigan

Published in the United States by Baker Books
a division of Baker Publishing Group
P.O. Box 6287, Grand Rapids, MI 49516-6287
www.bakerbooks.com

Published in the UK by the Society for Promoting Christian Knowledge

Printed in the United States of America

Library of Congress Cataloging-in-Publication Data is on file at the Library of Congress, Washington, D.C.

ISBN 10: 0-8010-1294-5 (pbk.)
ISBN 978-0-8010-1294-5 (pbk.)

Biblical quotations are either the author's own translation or are taken from the New Revised Standard Version of the Bible, copyright 1989, Division of Christian Education of the National Council of the Churches of Christ in the United States of America. Used by permission. All rights reserved.

Interior photographs of page fragments of the Gospel of Judas are copyright Kenneth Garrett.

Interior design by Brian Brunsting

For Nick Perrin

CONTENTS

Preface

On Friday, April 7, 2006, I began a 40-hour journey from Cairns, in northeast Australia, back home to the north of England. I had been lecturing for three weeks, and on holiday for three days. Now I was returning to take up my duties in the Diocese of Durham, starting with Palm Sunday, Holy Week, Good Friday and Easter Day itself.

The first newspaper I saw back in England mentioned two books that had been published that same Friday. They were about an ancient document called "The Gospel of Judas," which had apparently just been discovered and was now in the public domain. My first reaction, I confess—no doubt due to jet lag and the sense of a million other urgent things to do—was, "Not another new gospel!" I could see the whole scenario unfolding before me: newspapers and radio stations in uproar ("New Discovery Challenges Traditional Christianity"); soulful American scholars declaring that this new find would, in a very real sense, compel us to boldly go into questions the church had tried to cover up; general confusion in the general public ("But haven't the Red Sea Scrolls disproved it all?"); and, above all, a distraction from the real tasks facing the church at the start of the twenty-first century. I hoped, I confess, that the document would turn out either to be a forgery or to be so slight and uninteresting that I wouldn't have to bother much about it.

Wrong on both counts. Once I was back at the desk, the phone calls began. A moment of comedy: I tried to order the newly published "Gospel of Judas," only to have my local bookshop send me a novel by the same name (*The Gospel of Judas*, by Simon Mawer [London: Abacus, 2000]), which, like many others, exploits the excitement, almost the paranoia, that someone might turn up a document one day which would pull the rug out from under Christianity-as-we-have-known-it. (In the novel, the document turns out to be Judas's eyewitness account not only of the crucifixion but also of the corrupting of Jesus' body . . . in other words, no resurrection, no Christian faith.) I tried again online, and this time it arrived: *The Gospel of Judas*, edited by Rodolphe Kasser, Marvin Meyer and Gregor Wurst, with additional commentary by Bart Ehrman. I also obtained the wonderfully racy and journalistic account of how the original manuscript, having been discovered in the 1970s, was carted to and fro in search of a buyer, getting quite badly damaged in the process, before finally arriving nearly 30 years later on the desk of someone who could piece it together and translate it (Herbert Krosney, *The Lost Gospel: The Quest for the Gospel of Judas Iscariot*). Both books are published by National Geographic in Washington DC, which put out a TV documentary with the same participants, giving the clear impression that ancient Gnosticism is not only a fascinating topic for historians to study but also an exciting option which we badly need to revisit today.

Anyway, the document in question, the manuscript at the center of the excitement, appears to be genuine. Leading authorities in various fields, including carbon dating, have declared that it is an authentic manuscript from third- or fourth-century Egypt. And it is neither slight nor uninteresting. What's more, the comments from its first editors, particularly Meyer and Ehrman, are of very great interest, since they reveal precisely that longing for new evidence to set against classic Christianity which has become such a feature of American life in the last few decades. But the question I am left with is this: has the "Gospel of Judas" finally done to this whole movement, this whole modern enthusiasm for reconnecting with ancient Gnosticism, what, according to tradition, Judas himself did to his master? Has this extraordinary new document perhaps revealed, more clearly than the other similar writings we already knew, just what it was that the early "Gnostics" believed—and why it was that some of the greatest early Christian writers passionately rejected their alterna-tive message? Does it enable us to see, more clearly than before, just where the political, as well as theological, lines were being drawn in the second century? I think it does. That conviction has grown on me as I have stud-ied the document and what has already been written about it.

I am therefore writing this little book to make three points. First, this new "Gospel of Judas," while a spectacularly interesting archaeological find, tells us nothing about the real Jesus, or for that matter the real Judas. In particular, it doesn't (as some have claimed) "rehabilitate" Judas over against either the charges laid against him in the New Testament or the anti-Jewish use that was made of the Judas tradition in the Middle Ages. Second, the enthusiasm for this new "gospel" lays bare the real agenda which has been driving both what we might call the scholarly "Quest for an Alternative Jesus" and also the popular eagerness for such sensational material that we find in books like Dan Brown's *The Da Vinci Code*.[1] Third, the specific teaching of the "Gospel of Judas" only serves to highlight certain features about first-century Christianity that need to be drawn out more fully than is sometimes done. When we put these together we discover that the publication of this extraordinary find, over 1,500 years after it was written, reveals more strikingly than before the bankruptcy of the worldview it articulated and, by contrast, the compelling and attractive nature (not of much modern Western Christianity, we may grant, but) of the genuine Christian faith articulated in the New Testament, the faith for which those who opposed the second-century Gnostics suffered and died.

In an effort to keep the main text as uncluttered as possible, I have referred to the relevant works, scholarly and otherwise, in notes at the back of the book.

I am very grateful to Richard Bauckham, Richard Hays, Peter Head and Peter Rodgers, who commented on the first draft of this work at short notice and helped me sharpen it up. They are not, of course, responsible for my mistakes, but I am thankful both for their wisdom and for their encouragement. My warm gratitude, too, goes to Simon Kingston, Joanna Moriarty and the cheerful staff at SPCK. This is the thirty-third book of mine they have published in the last 15 years, and they continue to do a great job. Finally, Dr. Nicholas Perrin read the first draft and enabled me to profit greatly from his expertise in the field of second-century Gnosticism. Nick served as my research assistant from 2000 to 2003, and I dedicate this little book to him in belated gratitude and continued appreciation.

Tom Wright

1

Not Another New Gospel?

As an ancient historian, I am constantly frustrated at how little source material we possess. Some of the greatest writers from antiquity only survive in fragments. Even Tacitus, the magisterial historian of first-century Rome, has not come down to us complete. Some of Cicero's most important writings have only been preserved in part; some are lost altogether.

My oldest son, who is a modern historian, has the opposite problem. There are bulging libraries and archives all over the world, full not only of books but of newspapers, pamphlets and all kinds of artifacts, which can in principle illuminate the last two centuries of European history. I am jealous. I am one of those

17

people (today's generation might call us "sad") who feel bereaved when I think of the burning of the ancient libraries at Alexandria and Constantinople.

For this reason I rejoice at every fragment the archaeologists recover from the ancient world. I am startled when I visit Roman sites in North Africa and discover wonderful carved stones, often with detailed inscriptions, lying about in the long grass. (Surely, thinks the methodical Englishman, they should be cataloged and in a museum?) I am frustrated to stand on the large mound where a first-century earthquake buried the town of Colossae in western Turkey. (Why can't the archaeologists get their act together and persuade the Turkish government to let them excavate?) We historians want every coin, every scrap of parchment, every chunk of carved stone that could conceivably shed light on the fascinating, but frustratingly incomplete, story of the ancient world.

The publication of a new piece of evidence is therefore always a matter for celebration. Evidence is evidence. What we make of it is another matter, as we shall see; but the fact of a document emerging from the mists of history carries the same frisson as a mysterious stranger arriving on our doorstep with an unexpected and important-looking letter. We are instinctively, and rightly, eager to know what this new evidence is, where it came from, and how to interpret it.

That is the right spirit in which to approach the "Gospel of Judas." Before this astonishing document came to light, we only knew about the book from a few references in early Christian writings. Now we have it, at least in one version (there may have been others; we can't tell), and we can see what they were talking about. That is good news for the historian.

I begin in this way because I wouldn't want anyone to suggest that the church might try to hush up, or cover up, such a spectacular find. (Since I'm a bishop, we may as well be up front about this possibility.) The story of the Dead Sea Scrolls, which were discovered in 1947, has been full of accusations that the church was trying to hide them, to delay publication, to do anything to stop the truth leaking out, the truth that Jesus was after all an Essene, that early Christianity was just a strange Jewish sect . . . or whatever other theory was being invented at the time. In fact, of course (and despite the famous assertions by maverick scholars like Barbara Thiering and notorious novelists like Dan Brown), the Scrolls tell us nothing about Jesus, John the Baptist, Paul or any early Christians. They shed a flood of light on one small group within early Judaism, and on the text of the Old Testament that it used. That, in turn, helps us to understand some aspects of early Christianity, which was indeed in some ways a strange Jewish sect. But there was no cover-up; just the lengthy process, sometimes indeed culpably long but not theologically motivated, to piece together, edit and publish tiny fragments two millennia old. (The better-preserved scrolls were mostly published quite quickly.)

There have been several other hugely important ancient texts discovered over the last century or two. The Oxyrhynchus, Beatty and Bodmer papyri, together with other similar documents from Egypt, have not attracted the same kind of media excitement as the Scrolls, but are every bit as important for historians. They provide, for example, a second-century collection of the letters of Paul, known as "P46," and an (incomplete) copy of the Gospel of John dated around 200 ("P66"). Granted all the attention given to the Dead Sea Scrolls and the gnostic finds, it often comes as a surprise to people to learn that we have such early copies of books of the New Testament.[1]

But the other archaeological find that did hit the headlines was another discovery of the 1940s: the codices from Nag Hammadi in upper Egypt (a "codex" is an early type of book, as opposed to a scroll). These, like the Scrolls, took a long time to edit and publish, and for similar reasons. It was an immensely complex and difficult task. No accusations of ecclesiastical cover-up were made, because, unlike the Scrolls, the Nag Hammadi materials were not in the control of church-based scholars. And it is the Nag Hammadi materials that form the best background for this most recent publication.

In the case of the "Gospel of Judas," the 30-year delay between discovery and publication is explained, not by decades of painstaking scholarly work, certainly not (despite at least one press claim, in the British *Daily Mail*) by any attempt on the part of the church to hush it up, but by the comi-tragic vagaries of the antiquities market. Herbert Krosney tells the story of how the codex, originally discovered by illiterate peasants near the banks of the Nile in central Egypt, made its way to Cairo, and thence by an extremely circuitous route to a bank vault in New York, to Yale University, to an American dealer, then to Switzerland . . . and, at last, on to the desk of someone who knew both how to handle it and how to edit it. It is a fascinating tale of seemingly endless phone calls, plane journeys, bad deals, scholarly jealousy, intrigue, suspicion, hopes raised and dashed and raised again. In fact, it is as good a tale, in its own way, as the many novels that create similar, but fictitious, stories.

The gnostic "gospels," of which this "Gospel of Judas" is one, regularly speak of Jesus and his followers in ways that turn the heroes into villains and the villains into heroes. It is thus ironic to read what is in many ways an inverted version of this story, too (the story, that is, of the finding, haggling over, and eventual editing of this new text). This alternative version has been written by the man who would have loved to have edited the new find, but had to sit by and watch as someone else got there first: the leading American Nag Hammadi expert, Professor James M. Robinson of Claremont University.

His book *The Secrets of Judas*, published at the same time as the text itself, tells the story of its discovery, and of the skulduggery involved in getting it eventually into a laboratory and thence into print. But, instead of the sense of sustained excitement, and of a great project brought to a triumphant conclusion, Robinson makes the heroes into villains, and constantly portrays himself as the man who should have been playing the hero but wasn't even allowed on stage.[2] He writes in a scornful and dismissive tone of voice, and with rather too many exclamation marks. One detects a fair measure of what, in orthodox circles, might be called *odium theologicum*; perhaps, in the case of Robinson and his rivals, one ought to say *odium atheologicum*, the rivalry between different proponents of a worldview which rejects the "God" of Judaism and Christianity. The irony of Robinson's book is that, in order to produce it at the same time as National Geographic was publishing the "Gospel of Judas," he had to go to print without having been able to read or study the text he was discussing. We scan his work in vain for any account of the specific teaching of the new find.

Sadly, in the course of its wandering to and fro, being manhandled and stored in bad conditions, the papyrus codex deteriorated significantly. It became much harder to work on, and there are now frustrating holes where there should be continuous text. But what we have is still sufficient to justify the extravagant claims that have been made for the book. No, it doesn't disprove

Christian faith. But yes, it does tell us quite a lot about how some people in the second century were reinterpreting that faith. And the enthusiasm for texts like this tells us quite a lot, too, about how some people in the twenty-first century want to reinterpret it.

The codex in question, which was found, sold, stored, shipped to and fro and finally edited, actually contains more than the "Gospel of Judas," but this work is (to us at least) by far the most important part of it. The whole codex has become known as the Codex Tchacos, named after Frieda Tchacos Nussberger, the dealer who finally brought the book to Switzerland and passed it on to a proper scholarly editor. It also contains a version of the "letter of Peter to Philip," which we already know from Nag Hammadi;[3] a text entitled "James," consisting of a version of the "First Apocalypse of James," also known in Nag Hammadi;[4] and then, after the "Gospel of Judas" itself, a previously unknown book provisionally entitled "The Book of Allogenes."[5] An exciting find indeed, and one which will keep scholars busy for many years in further editorial and interpretative work.

Just in case anyone should smell a rat at this point . . . the experts are indeed fully and thoroughly convinced that the work really is genuine. It isn't a medieval or modern forgery. Carbon dating indicates that the present copy is from either the third or the fourth century, with the high probability being somewhere between AD 240 and 320.[6] The handwriting and the language itself—a local variation of Coptic, the familiar language of the Nag Hammadi documents—would be virtually impossible to forge. Most scholars assume that the work was translated from a Greek original, for the reason that the same assumption is normally made about the very similar texts from Nag Hammadi and elsewhere. We note in passing, however, as a point to return to, that a case can be made for Syriac, rather than Greek, as the original language of some of these documents. Nothing in what follows hinges on this point.

In particular, the document appears quite definitely to be the one referred to by the great theologian of the late second and early third centuries, Irenaeus, Bishop of Lyons, in southern France.[7] But, though it fits his description, it is hardly the kind of thing that would have been written by someone trying to forge a document to match his critique. It goes beyond it in various ways. This is what Irenaeus wrote:

> [Others again] declare that Judas the traitor was thoroughly acquainted with these things, and that he alone, knowing the truth as no others did, accomplished the mystery of the betrayal; by him all things, both earthly and heavenly, were thus thrown into confusion. They produce a fictitious history of this kind, which they style the Gospel of Judas.[8]

It isn't clear whether Irenaeus had actually read this work, or whether he had only heard about it. He goes on to say that he has made a collection of gnostic writings on other subjects, but he doesn't mention possessing a copy of the "Gospel of Judas." Nor does his description fit the work we now have in all respects, since the newly discovered document doesn't speak directly of "all things, earthly and heavenly, being thrown into confusion." Nevertheless, the mention of Judas as the only one who really understood the truth, and who therefore sent Jesus to his death, is dead-on. That is the central point that the "Gospel of Judas" was written to announce.

But why all the fuss? London-based journalist Damien Thompson, writing in the *Daily Telegraph*, declared that orthodox Christians preparing to celebrate Easter would be upset because this new document denied that Jesus rose again from the dead. Sundry other writers took it upon themselves to declare that here at last was a genuinely early document which showed that traditional Christianity was not all it was made out to be. That, of course, is what so many in contemporary Western culture are eager to hear; and that is why many people, seeing the report in the press and catching the drift of all the media hype, have responded, as I myself was inclined to, by saying, "Not another new gospel!"

But let me be clear. To repeat, I am delighted that we have yet more evidence about the ancient world, and about early reinterpretations of Jesus and of the Christian faith. The more we have, the better we can do our history. But the reasons why this book has been published in a snazzy dust jacket, carefully timed to catch the Easter market, and trumpeted around the media of the Western world, has nothing to do with making historical sources available, and everything to do with what, today, so many people passionately want to believe—and, it seems, passionately want to disbelieve. Touchingly, Herbert Krosney articulates what many instinctively want to think, and what they will use any scrap of evidence to support:

> This dating of the Coptic translation of the original Greek text makes the gospel's message even more compelling. If an entire sect believed that the great betrayal had in fact been ordered by Jesus and carried out by his favored disciple, that interpretation could, after study, become as valid as the version told in the New Testament.[9]

What precisely Krosney means by "valid" is an interesting point to which we shall return. But before we can take this story any further we must have a look at the wider world of thought within which (as everyone who has seen the text agrees) it really belongs. Who were the Gnostics, and what did they believe?

2

SECOND-CENTURY GNOSTICISM

Just when more people have begun to understand what "Gnosticism" might actually have been . . . some scholars are telling us to give up using the category altogether. It tries to take in too much, they say. It covers so many different movements, ideas and texts that it's no longer useful, and it can create more confusion than it solves. In any case, they suggest, it doesn't correspond to how the people we're talking about thought of themselves.[1]

Well, no doubt that kind of thing needs saying from time to time. Imposing loose and general categories on disparate groups, beliefs and writings can indeed become sloppy and unhelpful. Generalizations can, and often do, cause historians to distort the historical reality of both people and movements on the one hand and documents on the other. We constantly need to be on our guard against this danger. A decade or two ago there was a fashion for declaring that we could no longer talk about "first-century Judaism," only "first-century Judaisms," with the plural reminding us, somewhat sniffily, that there were of course many different varieties of Judaism, some of them bitterly opposed to one another, and that to lump them all together risked that kind of gross oversimplification. Some have made the same point about types of early Christianity: perhaps, they say, we should talk about Christianities, plural. Fair enough—up to a point.

But the existence of many variations doesn't mean there isn't something that they have in common. Unless the different types of Judaism were just that, types of Judaism, they couldn't constitute that plural category, Judaisms. And the same is true with Gnosticism. As we discover in the new book containing the "Gospel of Judas," leading scholars of the movement, such as Marvin Meyer and Bart Ehrman, are content to allow the label to stand. Provided we remind ourselves from time to time that, like postmodernism, or indeed the so-called "new perspective on Paul," there are as many varieties as there are people writing about it, and provided we allow each text to speak in its own voice and to stand on its own merits, there is no reason to avoid the general term. Irenaeus says that there were indeed some religious groups who actually referred to themselves as *gnostikoi*, "people of knowledge," and since he was controverting them it may be judged unlikely that he was making this up. Even if, like the word "Methodist," the term "Gnostic" was originally a label given by one group to another, who wouldn't have chosen it for themselves, it is still quite possible, indeed likely, that the term quickly became a useful marker for a general trend of thought and life, however much room for variation and improvisation there was within that broader movement.

The "Gospel of Judas" is in fact a remarkably clear expression of what for many years have been seen as the basic tenets of "Gnosticism." This particular work brings these tenets into sharp focus around a striking narrative: a dialogue between Jesus and Judas, climaxing in Jesus' command to Judas to hand him over to his death, and Judas's carrying out of this command. Marvin Meyer and Bart Ehrman both give commendably clear, succinct and accurate accounts of the worldview and beliefs in question, and the fourfold summary I shall now offer has no quarrel to pick with them.[2]

1. The most striking feature of Gnosticism, marking it out against the main line of Jewish and early Christian thought, is a deep and dark dualism. The present world of space, time and matter is an

inexorably bad place, not only a place where wickedness flourishes unchecked but a place which,
had it not been for an evil god going ahead and
creating it, would not have existed at all. The world
as we know it, in other words, is evil through and
through. What is more, human beings, consisting
as they do of physical matter, and living in this
wicked space and time, are themselves essentially
bad—unless, as we shall see, within this shell of
evil matter there lurks something very different.

2. This already points to the next main feature. The
world as we know it was made by a bad, stupid
and perhaps capricious god. There is another divine being, a pure, wise and true divinity who is
quite different from this creator god. Sometimes
this ultimate high god is called "Father," which is
confusing for Christians who associate that title
with the god who made the world. For Gnosticism, the god who made the world, along with
various other intermediate beings who may have
had a hand in the project at some stage, is at the
least misguided or foolish, and at worst downright
malevolent.

3. The main aim of any right-thinking human being,
therefore, will be to escape the wicked world, and
the outward human existence, altogether. "Salvation" means exactly this: attaining deliverance
from the material cosmos and all that it means.

Only so can one make one's way to the pure, higher spiritual existence where, freed from the trammels of space, time and matter, one will be able to enjoy a bliss unavailable to those who cling to the present physical world and who mistakenly worship its creator.

4. The final feature is not so immediately obvious, but it plays a central role in gnostic thought, and indeed is the feature because of which the word "gnostic" and its derivatives are appropriate designations. The way to this "salvation" is precisely through *knowledge*, "gnosis." Not just any old knowledge. Certainly not through knowing the sort of thing you might be taught in school, or for that matter in an ordinary church. Rather, this special *gnosis* is arrived at through attaining knowledge about the true god, about the true origin of the wicked world, and not least about one's own true identity. And this "knowledge" can only come if someone "reveals" it. What is needed, in other words, is a "revealer" who will come from the realms beyond, from the pure upper spiritual world, to reveal to the chosen few that they have within themselves the spark of light, the divine identity hidden deep within their shabby, gross outward material form.

A wicked world; a wicked god who made it; salvation consisting of rescue from it; and rescue coming through the imparting of secret knowledge, especially knowledge that one has the divine spark within one's own self. Those are the four distinguishing marks of Gnosticism as we find it, not only in the polemic of Irenaeus and other early Christian teachers, but in the texts themselves: the codices from Nag Hammadi and elsewhere, and now the "Gospel of Judas."

But there is more. Though this is difficult to track, not least because the texts we have use all kinds of coded language, there seem to have been different groups of "Gnostics," among whom of particular interest are the "Sethians." According to the Book of Genesis, Seth was the son born to Adam and Eve after Cain killed Abel.[3] For this particular group of Gnostics, Seth was the founder of a special "generation," the chosen ones, the sparks of light.

And, for some Gnostics at least, Jesus himself was seen as the "revealer." Hence the burgeoning of texts, many of which came to light at Nag Hammadi, which collect and arrange reported sayings of Jesus rather than stories about him. These books were referred to by their authors or editors as "gospels," though they belong, as we shall see, to a very different genre from the canonical gospels of Matthew, Mark, Luke and John. Sometimes these collections of sayings purport to be secret information imparted by Jesus to a favored few among the disciples. Sometimes they are special sayings supposedly delivered after Jesus had come back from the dead (though Gnosticism characteristically and unsurprisingly does not want to have anything to do with the *bodily* resurrection). All of them, in the nature of the case, are cast as teachings that will enable the recipients to attain the gnostic-style salvation, that is, escape from the wicked world by acquiring knowledge about themselves as sparks of light, about the origin of the world, and about the true god whom Jesus is revealing and to whom they already, in truth, belong.

One key feature of all such texts is their relentless hostility to the main lines of ancient Judaism—which is surprising, considering that not only do many gnostic texts use and reinterpret the Old Testament, but that many scholars believe (not least for that reason) that Gnosticism as we know it in the second century originated in Jewish circles. Be that as it may, these texts routinely pour scorn or even anger on the Jewish god, who is assumed (rightly, on the basis of the Jewish Scriptures) to be the creator of the world we live in. He is the evil, malevolent deity, completely different from the ultimate true god, and those who worship him are deceived, foolish and ignorant. As Bart Ehrman puts it, expounding the "Gospel of Judas" 39–40,

> the disciples who continue to practice their religion as if the ultimate object of worship is the creator god of the Jews, invoking Jesus' name in support of their worship, have gotten it all wrong. Rather than serving

the true God they are blaspheming him. And in doing
so, they lead their followers astray.[4]

Thus, whereas most Jews in the two centuries on either
side of the time of Jesus were emphasizing the kingdom
of God coming on earth as in heaven, and the justice
of God breaking in to history to make everything right,
rescuing the created order from its plight of corruption
and decay and giving to his people renewed (resurrection) bodies to live gloriously within this new world,
vindicated after their suffering on his behalf, the Gnostics were teaching precisely the opposite. The true god
whom they worshiped was, they believed, "completely
removed from this transient world of pain and suffering
created by a rebel and a fool."[5]

It may well be that it was out of the failure of the
various Jewish "kingdom"-movements in the two centuries either side of the time of Jesus that some Jews,
in sad desperation, began to reread their own traditions
in this upside-down way. Similar ideas surfaced again
much later, within that many-headed Jewish movement
known as Kabbalah. If we were to look for a particular
moment which might conceivably have precipitated a
new and strange way of reading the Jewish traditions,
and which could explain the rise, around the middle
of the second century, of the gnostic movements we
know from the writings discovered in Nag Hammadi and
elsewhere, and the writings attacked by Irenaeus and

others, there is an obvious proposal: the failure of the great revolt of Simeon Ben Kosiba, also known as "Bar-Kochba," "Son of the Star." The Romans crushed the revolt in 135, changing the face of Judaism forever.[6]

That might, as well, help to explain the almost cynical way in which the Gnostics read the Old Testament as if it were upside down. If events had appeared to demonstrate that YHWH, Israel's God, had led his people up a blind alley, and had allowed a great messianic figure (Bar-Kochba himself) and a wonderful rabbi (Rabbi Akiba, who had supported Bar-Kochba and declared him to be the Messiah) to get things so horribly wrong, maybe all the traditional perceptions of who were the good guys and who were the bad guys had to be stood on their head. Perhaps that is why, in many gnostic texts, the heroes become villains and vice versa: if the God of the Old Testament is after all a bad god who has let his people down, then maybe the people he disapproves of (such as Cain) were in the right after all, and the people he approves of (such as Abel) in the wrong. Thus the strange, topsy-turvy world of gnostic speculation takes shape. And thus, to the extent that Jews embraced Gnosticism as such, they were taking a giant step away from all that had been most characteristically Jewish, both in the Old Testament and in the so-called intertestamental writings, and all that continued to be said in the main line of rabbinic thought. (The rabbis, if one may risk a generalization in a vast and complex field, continued to affirm and invoke the one creator God, even though they no longer looked for his kingdom to come in the way that Akiba and others had hoped it would.[7])

But were the Gnostics in any sense Christian? Well, it depends what you mean. There has been much debate over the last century over the relationship between early Christianity and early Gnosticism. If it is true, as seems likely, that many whom we now know as Gnostics thought and spoke of themselves as Christians, as followers of Jesus, the historian should be prepared to allow at least that the word "Christian" may have been used in quite different ways by different people and groups. This is in fact highly likely.

One particular scholarly proposal, however, went considerably further than this, but is now largely abandoned. In the first half of the twentieth century many scholars tried eagerly to demonstrate that the early Christians, not least Paul and John, actually *derived* their mature theology, their interpretation of Jesus of Nazareth, from gnostic movements and ideas. The attempt to make that case has now largely fizzled out because of the massive counterevidence which shows that both John and Paul were deeply rooted in the Old Testament, and that they strongly affirmed the traditional Jewish creational monotheism which was precisely what the Gnostics rejected.

But since John, Paul and the other New Testament writers (and those they may be quoting in some of the early Christian hymns and poems embedded within their writings) do indeed speak of Jesus as being one with the eternal unique God, and of his coming into the present world to reveal the truth, it is not hard to see that this story could be extremely useful to anyone who wanted to propagate a very different worldview to that of John, Paul and the other first-century Christian writers. Keep Jesus as the key figure, a great and powerful teacher, one who has come from the other side to tell us what it's about and to rescue us from our plight . . . and simply adjust the nature of the plight (no longer sin, but materiality), the picture of God (no longer the creator of the material world, the God of Abraham, Isaac and Jacob, but a distant, pure being, unsullied by contact with the creation), the nature of salvation (no longer God's kingdom and justice coming to birth within the space-time universe, but instead the rescue of some humans from the material world altogether) . . . and, lo and behold, we are still followers of someone we call "Jesus," but we now have a worldview and a religion without those nasty Jewish bits. And, as we shall see, without any danger that the Roman authorities will take exception to us.

It is perfectly fair, therefore, to suppose that at least some of the Gnostics may indeed have considered themselves to be "Christian." Presumably Irenaeus and the other anti-gnostic writers would not have taken the trouble to oppose them at such length if they had not done so. They represented a threat; they were in danger of upsetting the faith of some, leading people into a different kind of faith, to worship a different kind of god, resulting in a different style of life.

What's more, it is likely that the first signs of this clash are visible within the New Testament itself. Paul refers contemptuously to a kind of "gnosis" which puffs you up, in contrast to love, which builds you up.[8] And whoever wrote the first letter to Timothy (many think the author was someone other than Paul himself, but it is certainly no later than roughly AD 100) warns the reader to avoid the "foolish empty chatter and contradictions of what is wrongly called 'gnosis.'"[9] Some, he says, have gone that route and have missed the mark in terms of the (true) faith.

Classic Gnosticism, of the type we find in Nag Hammadi and in the "Gospel of Judas," is in fact a hybrid. Its basic worldview is not Jewish, however much gnostic texts use, and reinterpret, ancient Jewish texts. Indeed, as we have already seen, it is profoundly anti-Jewish. In the same way, I shall argue in due course that it has very little to do with the actual message and mission of Jesus of Nazareth himself. But in a world of many gods, many religious movements, many philosophies (many of them varieties of Platonism, with its inherent dualism of spirit and matter), and many teachers combining ideas in ever new ways, it is not surprising that we find groups and writers seeking to use the name of Jesus to propagate and legitimize teachings very different from his own. It is not the last time in history that such a thing has happened.

All this brings us back at last to the new text that has caused all the fuss. What do we know about Judas Iscariot, and what does the "Gospel of Judas" do with this knowledge?

3

|

THE JUDAS OF FAITH
AND THE ISCARIOT OF HISTORY

|

The "Gospel of Judas" purports to be all about one disciple of Jesus in particular: Judas Iscariot. And the main thing that everyone knows about Judas Iscariot is that he betrayed Jesus. But did he? And, if so, why?

We need to take a long step back, right back toward the reasonably solid history of the early first century. The four canonical gospels agree that Jesus of Nazareth chose twelve special followers, presumably intending thereby to signal his reconstituting of the ancient people of God, the family of Israel, the twelve tribes based (at least notionally) on the twelve sons of Jacob.

Among these special followers, the canonical gospels tell us, were two who bore one of the most famous, the most glorious, names in Jewish history: Judah, the name of Jacob's fourth son. The form "Judas" is simply the Greek version of the same name. The name "Judah" actually means "praise"; Judah's mother, Jacob's wife Leah, declared when she bore him that now she would "praise" YHWH, Israel's God.[1] What's more, the tribe of Judah came to be seen as the royal family. King David came from Judah. According to ancient prophecy, that was the family from which the true kings of Israel would emerge.[2] One of the most famous Jewish leaders in the centuries before Jesus was Judas Maccabaeus; though he wasn't actually from the tribe of Judah, he had led an astonishingly successful revolt against the pagan Syrians and cleansed the Temple. That was enough to enable him to establish a dynasty that lasted a hundred years. The name probably helped as well.

We shouldn't be surprised, then, that many families named a son "Judah." First-century Palestinian Jews, in any case, seem to have had rather a shortage of boy's names, certainly by modern English or American standards. We know quite a lot about this through the massive researches of the Israeli scholar Tal Ilan, who has trawled through the mountains of evidence from ancient Jewish inscriptions, not least on tombstones and bone-boxes. These researches have been drawn on in turn by Richard Bauckham and others, who have elucidated their significance within early Christianity.[3] Interestingly, Jewish families tended not to use the names of the twelve original patriarchs, so much as those of the Maccabees (Mattathias, John, Simon, Judas, Eleazar and Jonathan).[4] In the index to the works of the Jewish historian Josephus, there are no fewer than 21 people called "Jesus," 29 called "Simon" and 15 called "Judas," with a further 4 called "Judes," another variation. One of Jesus' own brothers had the same name; some think he was the author of the "letter of Jude" in the New Testament itself ("Jude" being of course an Anglicized version of the same name, perhaps adopted to avoid saying "the letter of Judas").[5]

This explains why the particular "Judas" who betrayed Jesus was regularly marked out with a further name, "Iscariot," though there is no agreement as to what that word means (a member of the "Sicarii," the "dagger men," urban terrorists? A man from Kerioth? Perhaps even a retrospective word meaning "the betrayer"?). Most people in Palestine would know several people called "Judas," and, though the parents who chose the name might have been aware of its historic and patriotic overtones, in everyday life people would be as unlikely to think instantly of Judas Maccabaeus as people today, hearing of a person called "George," would be to think at once either of the English kings of that name or of George Washington.

We need to remind ourselves of this, because centuries of Christian sneering at the traitor Judas Iscariot
have left their mark, and the very name "Judas" (think
how different it would sound if we called him "Judah")
has become, tragically, a byword for betrayal. Those
of us of a certain age remember the moment when
someone shouted "Judas" at Bob Dylan for daring to
use an electric guitar on stage, thus betraying his folk
music heritage. And already, when the early Christians
told the story of Jesus and his followers, they arranged
the lists of disciples so that, whatever other variations
there might be, Judas Iscariot brought up the rear, with
a comment to the effect that he was the traitor.[6]

But of course during Jesus' lifetime, right up to that
awful moment in the Garden of Gethsemane, there
was no thought of Judas being a traitor. When Jesus
warned the disciples, at the Last Supper, that one of
them would hand him over to the authorities (betraying
the secret place where they used to stay on the slopes
of the Mount of Olives, a spot where the police could
arrest him with minimal disturbance), we do not find
the other disciples saying, "Well, we all know who that
will be," and pointing to Judas. Instead, we find them
genuinely alarmed and disturbed: "It's not me, is it?"[7]

In the same way, when the early church constructed
lists of "the Twelve" and put Judas at the end, with the
remark that he was the betrayer, there was no thought,
no hint, not the slightest suggestion, either that this

overtone was somehow carried by his name itself or that the name, and the fact of the betrayal, had anything whatever to do with being "a Jew." The very thought is ridiculous. Of course he was Jewish. So were all the others.

Why Judas did what he did remains unclear. It is tempting to try to place him on a rough map of first-century Jewish aspirations. The Pharisees longed for God's kingdom and hoped to speed up its arrival by energetic law-keeping. The Sadducees wanted to maintain the status quo. The Essenes retreated to the desert to follow the special teachings of their founder and wait for God's moment. The "fourth philosophy," sometimes loosely known as "zealots," positioned at what we might call the hard right wing of the Pharisaic movement, wanted to bring the kingdom by sacred violence, after the manner of Elijah, Phinehas and the Maccabee heroes, against the hated pagans and those who compromised with them. If Judas was a "dagger man," one of the "Sicarii," this would indicate that he was close to the last of these positions, but we cannot be sure.

Notoriously, the chief priests paid him 30 pieces of silver for his information and guidance, but though there was some other suggestion of his being too fond of money (Jesus had put him in charge of the common purse), it isn't clear that this was his only, or his main, motive.[8] At this point, all kinds of speculations have attempted to fill the gap: perhaps he did it because he really thought Jesus was going to mount a military revolution and get rid of the Romans, and he couldn't understand why, after the demonstration in the Temple, Jesus seemed to go on teaching instead of pressing home his advantage. Perhaps he was secretly jealous of Jesus; perhaps he hoped that, if Jesus was out of the way, another kingdom-movement would develop, and would need another leader, perhaps someone with a historic royal name . . . and so on. We don't know, and we probably never shall. The same is true of Judas's death: Matthew says he hanged himself, Luke that his stomach split open, and attempts to harmonize the two have seemed to most readers, starting at least with Origen in the third century, to be special pleading.[9]

The canonical gospels add a further spin: Satan, they say, entered into Judas and directed him to do what he did.[10] This doesn't simply mean "he was demon-possessed," as though his behavior then became evil in a merely random way. Rather, "the Satan" in Hebrew is the word for "the accuser"; in the book of Job, "the Satan" is the Director of Public Prosecutions in the heavenly court. Judas has a very specific "accusatory" role: he is the one who says "this is the man," precipitating the chain of events which ends up with Jesus being hauled before a kangaroo court and being condemned to death on trumped-up charges. Other mentions in the New Testament do not attempt to deal any further with the apparent theological problem that if it was God's will that Jesus should die for the sins of the world, and if Judas's betrayal precipitated that event, why was Judas still to blame? That is a problem we meet in many other spheres as well: one thinks of George Steiner's astonishing novel in which Adolf Hitler, discovered in the Amazon jungle by Nazi-hunters many years after the war and brought to trial, declares that, because through his actions the new State of Israel had come into being, maybe he was after all the Messiah . . .[11] The question of how God's intention that Jesus should die to bear the sins of the world is to be integrated with the wickedness of those who brought that death about is pressing for us; it clearly was not for the early church.[12]

What is quite clear from the gospels is that Judas's traitorous action has nothing whatever to do with his being Jewish. The suggestion is preposterous: Jesus was Jewish, all the disciples were Jewish, they moved in a largely Jewish world and were spearheading a very specifically Jewish-style kingdom-movement. They were claiming—it was the *raison d'être* of the whole movement—that the Jewish God was bringing in his kingdom, in fulfilment of ancient Jewish prophecies, through their mission. If anything, therefore, for Judas to try to do away with Jesus could just as well be construed as an anti-Jewish action, a desperate attempt to stop this Jewish-style kingdom-of-God movement in its tracks. That would be going too far, of course. The question of ethnic (let alone racial) prejudice is simply anachronistic in this setting.

But by the same token it only requires a moment's thought to show how ridiculous it is to suggest, as one leading Jewish apologist in the last generation did, that Judas Iscariot was himself actually a fictitious character, invented by the early Christians as a way of blaming everything on "the Jews." Equally, it is implausible to argue, as another scholar has done at length, that Jesus had selected Judas to be his go-between in arranging a secret confrontation with the authorities, and that things went badly wrong.[13]

In fact, there is no chance of Judas and his betrayal being a figment of early Christian imagination. He is far too closely woven into very early source material for that to be even a remote possibility. And (since there was no question until several centuries later of making him into a cardboard cutout "Jewish" hate-figure) there was no reason for the early Christians to cause themselves such embarrassment as to admit that the man who had betrayed Jesus had been one of the inner circle. No: Judas Iscariot is a figure of history, and though (as with many historical characters including some very recent ones) we cannot be sure that we understand his motives for acting as he did, there is no good reason to doubt that he really was one of the Twelve, or that he really did lead the authorities, under cover of darkness, to the place where he knew

Jesus could be found and arrested without causing a disturbance.

In view of the newly discovered "Gospel of Judas," it is interesting to note that there are several mentions of Judas in the early writings outside the New Testament that tend in the same gnostic direction. In all of them, however, the portrait of Judas is uniformly negative. The third-century "Acts of Thomas" has the devil boasting about having stirred up Judas to betray the Christ, and warns the reader against the covetousness which could bring one to a similar fate. Other legends from roughly the same period speak of Jesus encountering Judas in hell and rebuking him, since he had indulged in worshipping the devil under the guise of a snake.[14] This makes it all the more remarkable that the "Gospel of Judas" has turned things around and made Judas the hero. What sense can we make of this?

The key thing to realize as we approach the newly published document is that Judas is indeed the hero—but that the story is completely different. This is not the story of the God of Israel bringing in his kingdom on earth as in heaven, liberating Israel and inaugurating a new era of justice and peace for the whole creation. This is not the story of Jesus taking the weight of the world's evil on to his shoulders, dying to exhaust it and rising to launch God's new world. The "Gospel of

Judas" has no sense of a salvation that is *for* this world, but only of one that is *from* this world. In this "Gospel," Jesus himself is the first person who has to experience this "salvation," this release from the bondage of being human, of being trapped within a material body. *And Judas is the hero because Jesus commands him to help him experience precisely that.*

This is the particular—and utterly fascinating—spin that the new document puts on the whole story of Judas Iscariot. Unlike many of the gnostic "gospels," this book is more than a mere collection of Jesus' sayings. It has a definite plot with a specific resolution. But the plot is driven, not (as in Matthew, Mark, Luke and John) by the prophetic promises about God's coming kingdom, but by the gnostic ideology we studied earlier. From the beginning of the book a sharp distinction is drawn between two groups of people and the "god" they worship. It quickly becomes clear that the one group is the main body of disciples, who worship the creator god, the god of Israel, and that the other group consists, mainly at least, of Jesus and Judas. They know that the creator god, Israel's god, is a lesser being who can be denoted with contemptuous names like "Saklas" ("fool").[15] They belong to the "great generation," the "generation of Seth," that is, the people who have discovered that they possess the true divine spark within themselves, and who, enlightened by this knowledge, can sit loose to the affairs of the present world and look forward to a happily disembodied life hereafter, even if it means rejection in the present by those who still stupidly worship the creator god.

It is because of this that Jesus laughs at those who are still in ignorance. Much has been made of this feature of the "Gospel of Judas," and some have even tried to suggest that in this document, unlike the apparently sombre canonical gospels, Jesus has a sense of humor.[16] To reply, as some have done in the media, that the canonical gospels are in fact full of wry humor (camels going through needles' eyes, Jesus giving the disciples funny nicknames, and so on), misses the point. The reason Jesus laughs in the "Gospel of Judas" is not, as Meyer suggests, in a whimsical fashion "at the foibles of the disciples and the absurdities in human life," but because he is explicitly and scornfully mocking the disciples who are still worshipping the creator god, and doing so in the sacrament of the eucharist.[17] He laughs at them again for wondering about "the great generation," when in fact they will never attain it.[18] And he laughs, too, at the error of the wandering stars, destined to be destroyed, which presumably stand for, or perhaps influence, those humans who wander about in their this-worldly error.[19] I have to say that the attempt to reinterpret this in terms of a friendly, benign, joyful Jesus radiating divine wisdom, over against the gloomy suffering figure of the canonical gospels, is at best an exercise in special pleading and at worst a kind of wilful ignorance of what the text is actually asserting.[20]

It also ignores the mocking sense of laughter in the obvious parallel, in the Nag Hammadi text known as the "Apocalypse of Peter." There, the "real Jesus" laughs during the crucifixion because it is someone else, the merely fleshly "Jesus," who is being crucified as a substitute for him. Here the text is quite explicit: this "real Jesus" mocks and scorns the lack of perception of those who are "born blind," that is, the ordinary people who cannot see the "spiritual" truth. The laughter is sardonic; it is the reaction of the enlightened ones to those who do not share their insight.[21] A very similar point emerges in the book called *The Second Treatise of the Great Seth*, another Nag Hammadi text.[22] The Jewish scholar Guy Stroumsa summarizes the point like this:

> Jesus laughs at the sight of the stupidity of the "rulers"—the angels of evil. These act under the command of the god Saklas, who is the God of Israel, the creator of our material and evil world. Saklas and his cohorts intend to crucify Jesus, but they succeed only in killing the material body, an empty shell that the spiritual redeemer succeeded in exiting before the calamity. Therefore Jesus laughs.[23]

The strange thing is that Meyer, like Elaine Pagels, knows all this perfectly well.[24] Why, then, do he and others try to use the motif of laughter to make this

"Jesus" appear friendly and attractive? This is an important question, and I shall postpone the attempt to answer it until a later chapter.

All this serves to build up to the climax of the short work, which comes when Jesus tells Judas that his task will be to hand him over to the authorities, precisely so that in death he can escape this horrible world of materiality, of humanness, and become the spiritual being he really is:

> Jesus said, "Truly I say to you, Judas, [those who] offer sacrifices to Saklas . . . God . . . [three lines missing here] . . . everything that is evil. But you will exceed all of them. *For you will sacrifice the man that clothes me.*"[25]

"The man that clothes me" (or, as the editors say in a footnote, "the man that bears me"): that is the clue to it all, to the nature of the story in which Judas finds himself the hero rather than the villain. The editors' comment on this text is blunt and to the point:

> Judas is instructed by Jesus to help him by sacrificing the fleshly body ("the man") that clothes or bears the true spiritual self of Jesus. The death of Jesus, with the assistance of Judas, is taken to be the liberation of the spiritual person within . . . By making it possible for Jesus to die, Judas allows the divine spark within Jesus to escape the material trappings of his body to return to his heavenly home. Judas is the hero, not the villain.[26]

Whoever wrote this text, in other words, was doing with Judas, the apparent "villain" of the gospel story, what some other gnostic writers did for Cain, the apparent "villain" of the early chapters of Genesis. The worldview thereby expressed could hardly be clearer. What's more, it could hardly be less like the worldview that permeates the canonical gospels, and for that matter all the first-century Christianity to which we have direct access.

But there is more. Judas is to follow Jesus in due course. It will, of course, be uncomfortable for him; the other disciples will reject him, so that he will be seen as "the thirteenth," with someone else taking his place in the Twelve.[27] But the way by which Judas is to go will be through following his star, the star that is leading the way into the heavenly realm:

> And then the image of the great generation of Adam will be exalted, for prior to heaven, earth, and the angels, that generation, which is from the eternal realms, exists. Look, you have been told everything. Lift up your eyes and look at the cloud and the light within it and the stars surrounding it. The star that leads the way is your star.
>
> Judas lifted up his eyes and saw the luminous cloud, and he entered it. Those standing on the ground heard a voice coming from the cloud, saying . . . great generation . . . image . . .[28]

This has caused a certain amount of comment already, both on the ancient origins of the idea of each person (or at least each "enlightened" person) having a separate star and on its contemporary relevance. And, indeed, on the place of this scene within the narrative: Krosney declares that this moment is "equal in dramatic power to much that is in the canonical Gospels."[29] Meyer points out that the idea of individuals each having a "native star" belongs to the kind of cosmology we find in Plato's dialogue *Timaeus*. It has some affinities with the idea of "astral immortality," a popular notion in the ancient world as well as in the modern (when Princess Diana died, several of the tributes left to her expressed the belief that she had gone off either to join her own star or even to *become* a star).[30] But the real giveaway comment is that of Herbert Krosney, as he rounds off his fast-paced narrative of the finding and editing of the "Gospel of Judas." The message of the book, he says,

> turns the long-accepted belief that Judas betrayed his master on its head, and in so doing, it invites all of us to reexamine what Jesus tried to teach. Following our own star is an idea that is as relevant today as it was back then.[31]

There we have it: salvation by introspection, or perhaps salvation by Sinatra ("I did it my way"). Was it really, we may ask, worth all that trouble and expense just to hear a second-century writer saying what so many in North America and elsewhere already believe? I am reminded of the climax of the musical *Starlight Express*, where at the end it is revealed that "you have the starlight within you!"

That would, of course, be unfair to the text, which is much more subtle. But it already indicates something of the atmosphere, cultural and religious, in which the "Gospel of Judas" has been published, and something of the kind of question which we must put, as much to its interpreters as to the text itself. But before we do that, we must look at more of the "Gospel," and in particular at its cosmological speculations.

Even when Bart Ehrman, commenting on the "Gospel of Judas," is wanting to urge us to see the document as a splendid text worthy of close attention for its fresh insights, he is nevertheless forced to admit that some parts of it are "highly confusing and bizarre" and "befuddling."[32] A few lines will give the flavor (remembering that ellipses and square brackets indicate places where the text is lacking either wholly or in part):

> Adamas was in the first luminous cloud that no angel has ever seen among all those called "God." He . . . that . . . the image . . . and after the likeness of [this] angel. He made the incorruptible [generation] of Seth

appear . . . the twelve . . . the twenty-four . . . He made seventy-two luminaries appear in the incorruptible generation, in accordance with the will of the Spirit. The seventy-two luminaries themselves made three hundred sixty luminaries appear in the incorruptible generation, in accordance with the will of the Spirit, that their number should be five for each.

The twelve aeons of the twelve luminaries constitute their father, with six heavens for each aeon, so that there are seventy-two heavens for the seventy-two luminaries, and for each [of them five] firmaments, [for a total of] three hundred sixty [firmaments . . .]. They were given authority and a [great] host of angels [without number], for glory and adoration, [and after that also] virgin spirits, for glory and [adoration] of all the aeons and the heavens and the firmaments.[33]

When I first read this, and other passages like it, I had a stab of recognition. Here I confess, as it were, a personal interest: as a bishop, I regularly receive letters that sound exactly like this. Some are handwritten, in which case they are mostly in green ink. Some are typewritten, page after page of interminable cosmological speculation, with increasing amounts of block capitals and underlinings. Far be it from me to conclude that the author of the "Gospel of Judas" is to be put on a par with the ramblings of muddled minds in our own day. He only occasionally lapses into this stuff, and it may be partly redeemed by the knowledge that what seems obscure to us (though not, apparently, to some of my correspondents) may well have been familiar territory to his readers. (I am not so sanguine, however, about Meyer's explanation—or should I say apology?—for this kind of passage. He quotes Jorge Luis Borges's "Three Versions of Judas" to the effect that it was all a matter of politics: if Alexandria had won instead of Rome, this is the sort of thing we would all have been brought up on.[34]) But it does little to advance the implicit case, which Meyer and Ehrman and the others are trying earnestly to make against the odds at this point, that the "Gospel of Judas" is just the sort of thing we need today to help us set traditional orthodoxy aside and embrace something more interesting.

There are many other things that could be said about the document itself. But I will allow them to emerge piecemeal as we address the two main questions that are now before us. First, what are we to say about the relationship between this new "Gospel" and the canonical gospels—and the rest of early Christianity? And, second, what are we to say about the remarkably enthusiastic presentation of this new find by Meyer, Ehrman and their colleagues?

4

When Is a Gospel Not a Gospel?

When the "Gospel of Judas" was published, Dr. Simon Gathercole of Aberdeen University was quoted in the press as commenting that it was as though someone were to produce a document purporting to be a diary of Queen Victoria, in which she was discussing *The Lord of the Rings* and her CD collection. My own illustration, in a sermon preached six days after the book's publication, was similar: it is like finding a document which purports to be an account of Napoleon discussing tactics with his senior officers, but which has them talking about nuclear submarines and B52 bombers. In other words, anyone knowing the relevant history must realize that there is no chance of the "Gospel of Judas" giving us access to the genuine, historical figure of Jesus of Nazareth. Or, for that matter, to the genuine, historical figure of Judas Iscariot. What we are witnessing is a fictional character called "Jesus" talking to a fictional character called "Judas" about things that the real Jesus and the real Judas would not have understood—or, if they had, would have regarded as irrelevant to the "kingdom of God" which was the theme and purpose of their common life and mission.

This point is strikingly confirmed in the remarks made about the "Gospel of Jesus" by James M. Robinson, quoted in *Newsweek*, April 17, 2006. This new work, he declares,

> tells us nothing about the historical Jesus and nothing about the historical Judas. It tells only what, 100 years later, Gnostics were doing with the story they found in the canonical Gospels.

There may, to be sure, be some scholarly pique behind this comment—as appears from Robinson's next sentence, "I think purchasers are going to throw the book down in disgust." Robinson, as we saw earlier, and as emerges from Krosney's account as well as from Robinson's own book, was passionately eager to edit and publish the work himself, and bitterly disappointed that it went to the Swiss scholar Rodolphe Kasser instead.[1] But the fact that Robinson may have personal reasons for saying what he did doesn't mean it isn't true. The point is important; and it reflects, too, on the great majority of those texts which Robinson *did* collect and edit, that is, the Nag Hammadi codices themselves.

I have written at length elsewhere about Jesus of Nazareth in his historical context, and there is no need to repeat even a little of that material.[2] Even if details of my own sketch are controverted—and of course there will always be room for plenty of disagreement—the main line of Jesus-scholarship today has, I believe, largely left behind the fantasyland of the "Jesus Seminar" and its attempt to produce an "objective" portrait of Jesus while measuring the data against an already agreed reductionist framework. Likewise, it has not proved as easy as some thought it would be to construct a historically credible "Jesus" out of the fragments of the gnostic gospels such as "Thomas," even supposing them to be early, which many still doubt despite the powerful, and sometimes shrill, advocacy of the case in certain quarters. Jesus remains stubbornly and firmly a figure of Palestinian Judaism in the first third of the first century of the Common Era, not a teacher of strange, hidden wisdom after the manner of a Buddhist guru or a gnostic "revealer."

In particular, Jesus, and the movement he generated, remained passionately concerned about "the kingdom of God" in a sense that, although admittedly modified around his own particular vision and vocation, remains recognizably within the world of first-century Jewish eschatological and apocalyptic expectation. That is, Jesus believed, not that the world of space, time and matter was a gigantic blunder on the part of a secondary, incompetent and hostile deity, but that it was the world made by the God of Abraham, Isaac and Jacob, who was the one, true and only God, and that this God was bringing history—world history, Israel's history—to a great climax through which he would establish his sovereign and saving rule in and for the world. The coming of God's kingdom was never about people being snatched away from the wicked world to an otherworldly salvation. The prayer which Jesus gave his followers included, centrally, the petition that God's kingdom would come, and his will be done, "on earth as in heaven"—something which would have horrified any self-respecting Gnostic, and certainly the author of the "Gospel of Judas." We must bear this in mind in all that follows.

What can be said, then, about the comparison we are invited to make by the very use of the word "Gospel" itself—the comparison, that is, between "Judas" and Matthew, Mark, Luke and John—and for that matter "Thomas," "Philip," "Peter," "Mary" and the rest? This is a complex matter, and we have no space for detailed exploration. But some basic points must be made.

To begin with, the main contrast between the canonical gospels and the gnostic gospels is that the former are primarily narrative, with teaching interspersed within an overall storyline reaching a definite climax, while the latter (such as "Thomas") consist simply of a collection of sayings, arranged as much for the purposes of meditation or memorization as for any thematic sequence or continuity. To that extent, as I have often said in the past, the main difference is that, whereas the canonical gospels are *news*, Thomas and the others are *advice*. The canonical gospels tell a story of things that *happened*, through which the world has become a different place; "Thomas" and the others offer a list of musings, teachings, about how one might engage in a different practice of spirituality, and through this means attain disembodied bliss. To that extent, though the gnostic documents do sometimes call themselves "gospels," they manifestly belong to a different genre.

This point is made quite candidly by James M. Robinson, who has done more than most over the last half-century to edit, publish and interpret these texts. He writes:

> It is clear that the *Gospel of Thomas* was hardly designated by its original author or compiler as a *Gospel*. Rather he or she would have called it a collection of *sayings*. But then, in the effort to get it accredited by the church as being on a par with the *Gospels* gaining canonicity in the emerging New Testament, this collection of *sayings* was secondarily named a *Gospel*.[3]

This difference is not theologically or religiously accidental. The gnostic gospels, by and large, do not believe that anything has *happened* that has changed the world. They are not actually interested, as the canonical gospels are, in the events as events, in Jesus' biography as biography. (One of the great gains of New Testament scholarship in the last generation has been to reestablish that the canonical gospels certainly were intended, and certainly are to be read, within the framework of ancient biographical writing. They are more than that, but they are certainly not less.[4]) Whatever the "Jesus" of these gnostic "gospels" has done, the main thing about him is that he has come, not to rescue the world, or to heal or change it, but to give secret teaching about how to escape it.

In particular, neither of the two obvious meanings of "gospel" in the first century are relevant for the Gnostic. The reference back to Isaiah's messenger of good tidings, coming to tell Jerusalem that her long suffering was at an end and that God was coming back to be king at last, is precisely what the Gnostic does not want to hear.[5] And the wider first-century use of "gospel," as a proclamation about Caesar and his empire, was singularly irrelevant as well. In fact, as I shall suggest presently, that may have been part of the point.

All this remains true, and a glance through any of the collections of the gnostic "gospels" will confirm the point: normally, they are collections of teaching, rather than sustained narratives. Yet there are exceptions to this rule, and the "Gospel of Judas" is, to some extent at least, one of them. (We should also mention the existence of other "gospels" that are more like the canonical ones. For example, the "Gospel of the Nazarenes" seems to have been quite orthodox in its theology; at least Jerome, who mentions it, thought so.)

Another exception to the rule of non-canonical "gospels" being collections of teaching is the so-called "Gospel of Peter," which fits neither into the "Thomas" bracket nor into that of the canonical gospels. It offers a strange, somewhat surreal variation on the passion and resurrection narratives of the canonical gospels (attempts to argue for its independence are now generally regarded to have failed). It contains elements that some have seen as gnostic (Jesus feels no pain on the cross) and has a strong, consistent and overarching anti-Jewish tendency which, as we have seen, can likewise belong with Gnosticism due to its devaluing of the material world.[6] In particular, and in sharp contrast to the canonical gospels, "Peter"—precisely because it does not place any positive value on the Jewish story or the biblical prophecies—has no explanation of why the events of Jesus' death and resurrection actually *accomplish* anything, unless it be to demonstrate the guilt of the Jewish people and their deserving of punishment. The one thing that is achieved, according to "Peter," is that Jesus has "preached to those who are asleep."[7] But what precisely this means, where the idea has come from, and how in any case Jesus' crucifixion accomplished this "preaching," all remains unclear. "Peter" is, then, "news" in the sense that it is an account of things that happened, including an extraordinary resurrection scene with Jesus coming out of the tomb supported by two others, and being followed by the cross. But there is no explanation in the text as we have it (granted, of course, that as it stands it is fragmentary) of why this might be *good* news, "euangelion," "gospel."

Here, it might be thought, the "Gospel of Judas" could make a new contribution. And in a sense it does. If it is indeed true that the material world is a place of wickedness, sorrow and disaster, and that the one thing humans need to do is to escape both from it and from the god who so stupidly made it, then it might be considered "good news" that Jesus should have commissioned one of his friends to hand him over to his death—not so that he could die for the sins of the world, but so that he could lead the way out of the material world altogether and off into the disembodied heavens.

That is precisely what is claimed by those who have edited, and commented upon, the "Gospel of Judas." Judas's betrayal of Jesus, instead of being the prelude to the climax as in the canonical gospels, is itself

the climax of this account: not Jesus' death and resurrection, but the faithful act of his most intimate com-
panion and faithful follower, the one who handed him
over to his death that he might return to his heavenly
home.[8]

Judas, having been commanded to "sacrifice the man
that clothes me," could "do no less for his friend and
soul mate, and he betrays him. That is the good news of
the Gospel of Judas."[9] But the implicit larger narrative
of which this is then the climax is, quite obviously, un-
ambiguously and uncontroversially, not the story which
first-century kingdom-seeking Jews were telling, the
story of the God of Abraham making promises through
his prophets, promises about liberating Israel and bringing his kingdom on earth as in heaven, but rather the
story which second-century Gnostics were telling, the
story of a higher god who trumps the wicked, world-
creating god of Israel and enables some humans, led by
a mysterious revealer-figure, to discover the true divine
light within themselves and so to be liberated from the
created order, and the created physical body, and all
the concerns that go with the material world. To this
extent, and seen from the perspective of the canonical
gospels, the "Gospel of Judas" is an *anti*-gospel: a story
about the arrival of news which is only good if you
have stood the world on its head. It is like a messenger
coming smiling into the prison camp to say that the war

has been won—only to reveal that the *other* side has won, and that all the prisoners are to be killed.

To set "Judas" alongside Matthew, Mark, Luke and John, then, is to discover quite quickly what it is that they have which none of the gnostic gospels have: a tripartite theme which runs through them all, in different but theologically coherent ways.

First, they are recounting how the long story of God and Israel came to its God-ordained climax—meaning by "God," of course, the creator God, the God of Abraham, Isaac and Jacob. The canonical gospels have various ways of doing this, both in form and in content, but it is a major theme for each of them. And this is of course precisely one of the things that the gnostic gospels, including "Peter" and "Judas," were concerned to eliminate absolutely. "Thomas" and the other sayings-collections eliminate it structurally, since there is simply no larger story line, no hooking in to the history of Israel, no sense of long-awaited promises coming at last to fulfilment. In addition, "Thomas" and the others sometimes indicate their desire to eliminate it in actual content: "I will destroy this Temple," says the "Jesus" of "Thomas," "and nobody will be able to build it."[10] Judaism and its institutions are irredeemable. At this point there is simply no common ground between the gnostic gospels and their canonical predecessors.

Second, the canonical gospels are telling the story of Jesus in such a way as to lay out the ground plan for the ongoing life of Jesus' followers, those on "the Way" (as it was called early on), those who became known as "the Christians," i.e. "the Messiah's people." This is the truth underneath the old, overemphasized point of the form critics: that the material in the gospels, both the small units and the larger editorial plans, were shaped, at least in part, by the needs of the emerging church.

This is not to say that the material was created for this purpose out of whole cloth. I and others have argued the point elsewhere. There is far too much historical coherence, and far too significant an absence of other themes which should have been included had that been the driving force, for that theory to hold. An obvious example is the topic of circumcision: we know that it was one of the fiercest and most difficult controversies in the early church, but nobody ever thought to invent a "saying of Jesus" which addressed it.[11] But it remains quite obviously the case that the stories of Jesus have been told simultaneously to say not only, as in the first point above, "this is how the story of Israel reached its climax," but also, "these are the events which generated, and continue to sustain and shape, the life of the Christian movement."

Once again, the gnostic gospels are extremely keen not to tell any such story. Of course, there is a shadowy parallel: they are telling, supposedly, the story of how Jesus in fact gave all kinds of secret teaching to select disciples, teaching which was then passed on by word of mouth to those "in the know." But the gnostic writings are designed to say, among other things, that "Jesus" and his teaching did *not* validate or shape the life of the mainline church as it was then developing through the teachers and leaders of the post-apostolic age such as Ignatius, Clement, Polycarp, Justin and the rest. "Judas" explicitly and scornfully rejects the emerging church and its practices, comparing them to those who engage in immorality and violence.[12] The gnostic gospels, in other words, are very careful not to tell the story of Jesus in any way that would provide grounding for the proto-orthodox church.

Third, obviously but importantly, the canonical gospels tell the story of Jesus himself, and do so in such a way as to make the claim, on page after page, that it was through his life, public career, death and resurrection that God's kingdom was indeed launched on earth as in heaven. This claim has, of course, been variously controverted. Many Jewish people from that day to this have commented that of course the kingdom hasn't come, because the world is still full of wickedness—to which the Christians have regularly replied, as Jesus himself seems to have done, that the kingdom is coming like a seed which will bear fruit, rather than in a single flash of lightning. But the flashes of lightning are there, too, and they matter; and it is unthinkable that the canonical evangelists were not profoundly aware of the question. Their answer, consistent (as I have argued elsewhere) with the mind-set of Jesus himself, is that for God's kingdom to come the Messiah had to fight the great battle with evil, and thus emerge triumphant, launching God's new world, the world in which death itself had been defeated. It is because the evangelists believed this that they tell the story the way they do.

And that, once more, is what the gnostic gospels, for obvious reasons, are anxious to avoid. They do not see Jesus inaugurating God's kingdom in any sense that a first-century Jew would recognize, not even in the carefully modulated sense which Jesus himself articulated. They certainly do not see his death as accomplishing any kind of victory, except the kind of victory imagined in "Judas," where the body is happily allowed to die so that the spirit may fly free. And they do not, they most emphatically do not, believe in Jesus' resurrection. It has been utterly reinterpreted. For the first century after Jesus' death, all references to resurrection meant what that word meant in the wider classical world (where the concept was known, but firmly denied) and the wider Jewish world (where a majority, following the Pharisees, believed in it): that is, a new bodily life after a period of being bodily dead.[13] (That is why, incidentally, it was so ridiculous for the newspapers to make a fuss over a newly published gnostic gospel that denied, or more exactly ignored, the resurrection. You might as well expect President Bush to include Texas in his list of states that constitute an "axis of evil." Of course he wouldn't include Texas; of course the Gnostics wouldn't want a resurrection.)

One last contrast between the canonical gospels and the gnostic ones. There is no point dressing it up: the canonical gospels are early, and the gnostic ones are late. (By "early" I mean within a generation or so of the death of Jesus; by "late" I mean no earlier than around the middle of the second century.) Howls of protest arise when one says this sort of thing, but all the signs point to this as the correct analysis.

Granted, we simply do not know exactly when the four canonical gospels were written. Some brave souls still try to suggest that we (or at least they) actually do know, but it is remarkable how imprecise the actual arguments are, and how much latitude the documents will allow. It is highly likely that Mark at least was written well before AD 70, and it is highly unlikely that Matthew, Luke and John were written any later than 80, or 90 at the outside. There is actually no very good reason why they might not all be considerably earlier. The old scholarly "consensus" for a relatively late date has been whittled away from most angles over the last generation, though the older critical orthodoxy continues to be taught, like the grin on the Cheshire Cat when the rest of the Cat had disappeared. But again we simply do not know.

What we do know is that by the time Ignatius of Antioch was writing his letters, in the first decade or so of the second century, he is quoting sayings of Jesus that we now find in the canonical gospels, especially in Matthew and John. It isn't clear whether he knows these sources as oral or written; but he certainly knows plenty of sayings of Jesus that we now find in our written canonical gospels, and it is clear that he regards them, and presumes that his readers regard them, as authoritative. The popular notion that there was no such thing as a recognized collection of biblical books until the third or even the fourth century, but that all kinds of documents were circulating in an undifferentiated mass until political expediency suggested the selection of those books that would make a particular point, is simply rubbish, as James Robinson already tacitly admits in the passage about "Thomas" already quoted. The canonical gospels were being read and quoted as carrying authority in the early and middle second century, whereas we do not even hear of the non-canonical ones until the middle or end of that century. Attempts to postulate early (in some cases very early) versions of some of the gnostic texts such as "Thomas" or "Peter" have not commanded much general assent outside a vocal North American minority. Indeed, strong arguments have recently been advanced to show that, despite the desperate attempts to push "Thomas" into the early years of the second century or even all the way

back into the first, the high probability is that it, like
the other Nag Hammadi documents and the "Gospel of
Judas" itself, was composed or compiled in the middle
or late second century.[14]

I have no problem with saying that some of the non-
canonical gospels may well preserve, here and there,
genuine memories of Jesus that have not survived elsewhere. Even within a short public career it is highly
likely that Jesus said all sorts of things which are not
collected together in the canonical gospels; John, indeed, says as much, and Acts records one saying of Jesus
which appears neither in Luke nor anywhere else.[15]
But the gnostic gospels, so called, do not constitute a
genuinely independent witness. They are, again and
again, manifestly derivative from the canonical tradition. This point has been made often enough, though
it is still resisted in many quarters. (A typical argument runs like this: where "Thomas" contains parables
like those in the synoptic gospels, it misses out on the
"allegorical" interpretation; therefore it represents an
earlier stage in the tradition, before the church had
"allegorized" Jesus' simple though profound sayings.
Answer: the parables in question belong in fact demonstrably within the Jewish apocalyptic tradition in
which a quasi-allegorical narrative plus interpretation
would form a single indivisible whole, so that what has
happened is that someone in the second century has,
by removing the interpretation from the original form,

swapped a first-century Jewish apocalyptic worldview for the teaching of gnomic wisdom.[16]) It would take a much longer study to argue this out in proper detail, but the key fact has to do with the character of the different writings.

Here are the alternative historical possibilities.

1. A movement which began as a first-century Palestinian Jewish kingdom-of-God movement, couched in apocalyptic language and imagery designed to refer to coming great events and invest them with their theological significance, quickly gave rise to a literature which preserved this perspective, but then gradually gave birth, through transplantation into different cultural and philosophical soil, to a different worldview and literature in which some of the same language was being used but in which the worldview in question was that of Hellenistic dualism.

2. Jesus of Nazareth really did teach a kind of Gnosticism, or even (as is sometimes suggested) a kind of Buddhism, a spirituality of self-discovery on the one hand and escape on the other, and this was then translated by the canonical evangelists and/or their sources into a fictitious first-century Palestinian Jewish kingdom-of-God movement, complete with remarkably well fitting and dovetailed traditions about the extraordinary human

being at its center, while the true message of, and about, Jesus was preserved in traditions which in other respects bear all the hallmarks of a Hellenized, Platonized second-century movement.

As a historian I find the first of these sequences credible and natural, the second incredible and forced. When I meet that sort of choice elsewhere in my work—or, indeed, in ordinary life—I know which way to go.

All this merely underlines the points made above about the radical differences in character and genre, as well as theology, between the canonical gospels and their distant gnostic relations. The utter incompatibility of the two portraits of Jesus, the canonical one and the gnostic one, gives the lie to the suggestion, already put about in the literature on "Judas," that the two types are basically complementary. Elaine Pagels, one of the leading scholars of early Gnosticism and one of the greatest proponents of a "gnostic"-style Jesus, suggests that one might read the canonical and the gnostic gospels alongside one another, employing the canonical text for public, basic-level teaching and the gnostic one for private, advanced-level teaching. The gnostic texts, she suggests, were treasured because they were for people who were looking for deeper levels of spiritual discipline and understanding. It is on this basis that Herbert Krosney, drawing on Pagels, suggests that "the Gospel of Judas offers an alternative narrative, but does not challenge the bases of Christian faith. Instead, it may augment that faith by providing an additional view of the personality of Jesus."[17] Pagels is in fact here simply echoing the position which she herself has shown to be that of the western branch of Valentinian Gnosticism, represented by teachers such as Ptolemy and Heracleon, and documents such as the "Interpretation of the Knowledge."[18]

One can perhaps make allowances for Krosney, an award-winning documentary filmmaker rather than an ancient historian, in failing to appreciate the difference between the canonical and the gnostic gospels. But Elaine Pagels's statement is quite breathtaking. It could only be sustained by a systematic and sustained rereading, and in fact a radical misreading, of the canonical gospels themselves. When it all comes down to it, Matthew, Mark, Luke and John believed that Jesus really was Israel's Messiah, and that he had indeed come to bring about the kingdom of the one creator God on earth as in heaven. "Judas," like "Thomas" and the other gnostic texts, believed that that would have been a disastrous mistake, and that Jesus had come to show the way out of Judaism, out of the wicked created order, and off into a different realm altogether. Pagels is actually well aware of this, as her own summary indicates:

Uninitiated Christians mistakenly worshiped the creator, as if he were God; they believed in Christ as the one who would save them from sin, and who they believed had risen bodily from the dead: they accepted him by faith, but without understanding the mystery of his nature—or their own. But those who had gone on to receive *gnosis* had come to recognize Christ as the one sent from the Father of Truth, whose coming revealed to them that their own nature was identical with his—and with God's.[19]

These two sets of belief are like oil and water; like chalk and cheese. If we cannot see that, we are simply not paying attention to the texts. The idea that there might be a progression from the first to the second, as with basic and advanced teaching of the same subject, is simply wishful thinking, whether in the second century or today.

In short, "Thomas," "Judas" and the rest may indeed have called themselves "gospels" (though, as we have seen, some scholars like Robinson doubt that this was how their original authors regarded them). But, once they do that, or once someone attaches that label to them, the word itself changes its meaning. For the earliest Christians, the word "gospel" was on the one hand rooted in the Old Testament, and was on the other hand confronting a very different "gospel" out on the street. That very different "gospel" was the "gospel" of Caesar. This is where we discover what is perhaps the most telling point of difference between the Gnostics (however much they may have thought they were revering Jesus) and the Christians represented by people like Ignatius, Justin and Irenaeus. To explore this shall need another chapter.

5

LORD OF THE WORLD
OR ESCAPER FROM THE WORLD?

I said that the canonical gospels contained three stories, and so they do: the story of Israel reaching its
climax; the story of the emerging church being launched
through the work of Jesus; and the story of Jesus himself
inaugurating the kingdom of God—of Israel's God!—
through his public work, his death and his resurrection.
But there is another story hovering in the background,
a story of an ancient confrontation reaching its climax
after centuries of standoff and skirmish.

This is the story of the creator God, the only God,
the God of Israel, on the one hand, confronting on the
other hand the gods who claimed to rule the present

world—more particularly, the gods who claimed to be masters of the world through their agents, or even their embodied selves, in the persons of emperors and tyrants. It is the story of YHWH and Babylon, as seen by Isaiah 40–55; of Daniel in the lion's den, and of the monsters and the "son of man" in Daniel 7; of the heaven-sent victory of Judas Maccabaeus over the Syrian megalomaniac; of Rabbi Akiba and his noble but futile support for "Bar-Kochba," the "son of the star," as the last best hope of Israel against the might of pagan Rome. This is one of the central Jewish stories; it is what Jewish "kingdom of God" language is basically all about; it is part of the implicit background plot of all four canonical gospels.

In the middle of this story, blindingly obvious to almost everyone in the first century and astonishingly opaque (so it seems) to almost everyone in the twenty-first, is the story of Jesus and Caesar. If Jesus was announcing God's kingdom, he knew, the disciples knew, the chief priests knew, Herod knew, and ultimately Pilate knew (though all of them were muddled and puzzled to a lesser or greater extent), that this had something at least to do with a transfer of power and authority. Caesar, like many ancient tyrants, claimed divinity or at least quasi-divinity ("son of god," since emperors were routinely divinized by their heirs and successors immediately after their death). Caesar's accession and his birthday were occasions of "good news": *euangelion* in Greek, the same word as in the New Testament. Rome itself was deified, and like any self-respecting goddess she claimed to confer blessings on her devotees—justice, freedom, peace, salvation, the usual imperial boasts. If Jesus was talking about God's kingdom coming on earth as in heaven, then whatever he meant by that (and he spent a good deal of time "explaining" it in parables which were themselves, it seems, designed to be cryptic, to keep people guessing and so to keep danger at bay for the moment), the one thing he did *not* mean was "here is a new form of spirituality which will enable you to discover a divinity deep within yourself and thereby to escape from the problems, and the power plays, within the present wicked world."

Nor did the early church draw back from the conclusion that Jesus' message and accomplishment was to be seen in terms of the ancient Jewish confrontation of the kingdom of God and the kingdoms of the world. Matthew's risen Jesus declares that all authority in heaven *and on earth* has been given to him; that is the basis on which he sends out his followers to make disciples, to baptize and to teach. Mark's Jesus declares that the "gospel" must be proclaimed to all the nations—in a world where there already was a "gospel" going around the Mediterranean world, namely the "good news" of Caesar. Luke's Jesus commands his followers to announce a new way of life to all nations, beginning from Jerusalem, and he continues the story until the emissary of this "gospel" arrives in Rome and preaches there, under Caesar's nose, "openly and unhindered." John's Jesus stands before Pilate, Caesar's representative, and declares that he is indeed a king, though not of the same type as Caesar. His kingship is not *from* this world; that is, its origin is from elsewhere; but it is certainly *for* this world.[1] And John's gospel ends, as they all do only more so, not with an escapist spirituality embodied by Jesus and now to be imitated by his followers, but with the note of creation renewed and of Jesus as its Lord and God.[2]

This same theme is picked up again and again by Paul, as I have argued in detail elsewhere.[3] For Paul, Jesus is Lord and therefore Caesar is not. Paul's attitude to the imperial authorities has often been misunderstood, because Romans 13:1–7 has been read out of context and without regard to the multiple signals elsewhere in that letter, let alone in Philippians and 1 Thessalonians where the theme is clear and pronounced. It is Paul who takes the word "parousia," "royal appearing," which, unlike so many of his key terms, is not drawn from the Greek Old Testament, and uses it to hold together (a) the Jewish belief in the "day of the Lord," now rethought around Jesus, and (b) his belief that Jesus was upstaging Caesar.

"Our citizenship is in heaven," he wrote in Philippians. But he didn't mean "and so we must find the best and quickest way of going off there and leaving behind this wicked world and our wretched bodies." That isn't how the logic of citizenship works. Rome planted colonies, often of old soldiers, not so that they could return to their mother city when they retired from work but precisely so that they wouldn't; their task was to bring Roman influence to bear on the countries and societies where they were. And if they got into difficulties in the process, Caesar would come from Rome, not to scoop them up and take them back home safely, but to transform their situation by subjugating all possible enemies with his unstoppable power. Yes, declares Paul, "our citizenship is in heaven, and *from there we await the savior*, the Lord, the Messiah, Jesus, who will change our lowly bodies to be like his glorious body, by the power which enables him to subject everything to himself."[4] That is the exact opposite of Gnosticism, and with exactly the opposite effect. The Gnostic can escape from political confrontation into the world of private spirituality. The Pauline Christian must trust the world's true Lord and stay to see the thing through, even, if necessary, at the cost of martyrdom.

Martyrdom, naturally, came soon enough for those who embraced this early, Jewish, first-century, Jesus-based vision of God's kingdom coming on earth as in heaven.

The classic example from within the New Testament is the book of Revelation. Over and over again the writer, addressing a situation where many Christians have already been killed and many more face likely death, employs the language and imagery of the Old Testament and of Jewish apocalyptic in order to declare that Caesar's kingdom was a sham and that the God who made the world, the single God whom all creation worships, was taking forward his age-old plan to win his wonderful creation back from the usurping powers of evil, not least the powers of pagan empire. The book is of course long and complex, but one thing is crystal clear: the final vision, of the New Jerusalem *coming down from heaven to earth*, is both the utter rejection of any kind of gnostic soteriology on the one hand and the ultimate statement of political intent on the other. Jesus is "king of kings and lord of lords," and, in Paul's phrase, at his name every knee shall bow.[5]

Of course, the same books which speak so clearly of God's kingdom coming on earth as in heaven (once we have learned to read them the way a first-century reader would read them, instead of emasculating them by the artificial split between "religion" and "real life" that has been fashionable for the last two hundred years) also speak, equally clearly, of the totally different *kind* of kingdom, the completely different type of power, which this involves. It isn't the case that Jesus has the same sort of power as the rulers of the world, only quite a bit more of it. It is, rather, that he is embodying and enacting a different sort of power, a different sort of kingdom, altogether. That is the point which many, not only the proponents of Gnosticism but also those who just prefer a quiet life, have seized on in order to say, "Ah yes; that's because Jesus came to bring a *spiritual* kingdom, not a political one."

But the passages I have already quoted rule out that conclusion—as if it were not already ruled out by the history of the church in the first two centuries, which could easily have employed such an excuse had it been available, and thereby saved itself a good deal of trouble, tears and blood. The "spiritual" kingdom which Jesus did indeed come to bring was the spirit-empowered inbreaking rule of the one true God *into* the created world which, though spoiled by rebels, yet remains his, and yet remains beloved. The greatest theme of Paul's greatest letter is precisely God's justice, God's longing to put the world right once and for all, bringing with it a promise of salvation not *from* the world but *for* the world.[6] But that promise generates and sustains, not the normal type of political or military revolution, but a cheerful celebration of the victory of Jesus the Messiah over death itself, the tyrant's last weapon, so that the very cross which had been the symbol of Caesar's hated rule now becomes the symbol of the unsearchable depths of love at the heart of the creator God, Israel's God. And victory over death does not mean colluding with death, regarding death itself as a friend, as does the "Gospel of Judas." Victory over death means regarding death as the ultimate enemy, defeated by Jesus and no longer able to terrify.[7]

That is the theology that sustained the church through the early years of persecution. A quick glance through Ignatius of Antioch (who died around AD 110) makes the point; people sometimes talk as if Ignatius were interested solely in his own episcopal power and prestige, whereas the truth of the matter is that he was following his crucified Lord in the full knowledge of where that would all too quickly lead him. Polycarp, Bishop of Smyrna, in the first half of the second century, is quite clear about the confrontation between two rival masters: "Eighty-six years I have served him," he says to the official who is trying to make him denounce Jesus, "and he has never done me any wrong; how can I blaspheme my king who saved me?" Polycarp knew full well that "king" and "savior" were Caesar-titles, and that his statement of loyalty to Jesus would lead straight to the stake.[8] So too with Justin Martyr: broad in his sympathies, ready to listen and enter into dialogue, but when required to give allegiance to Caesar rather than Jesus he refuses point blank.[9]

In particular—and this is of more than passing interest for our story—there are the martyrs of Vienne and Lyons. A near-contemporary account of the horrific sufferings of the Christian community in those two leading cities of Gaul is preserved in the later *History of the Church* by Eusebius.[10] The persecution, supported by the emperor in Rome, swept through the cities, seeking out Christians right, left and center, accusing them (as does the "Gospel of Judas") of all sorts of immoral wickedness—unnatural sexual practices, cannibalism, and the like. The persecutors, it appears, made a special point of burning the bodies and scattering the ashes into the river Rhone, so that nothing of them would remain. Then comes the telling point:

> And this they did as though they could conquer God and take away their rebirth, in order, as they said, "that they might not even have any hope of resurrection, through trusting in which they have brought in strange and new worship, and despised terrors, going readily and with joy to death. Now let us see if they will rise again, and if their God be able to help them and to take them out of our hands."[11]

These martyrdoms took place in Vienne and Lyons in AD 177. Among those who died was the 90-year-old Pothinus, Bishop of Lyons, who was tortured to death in prison. And it was immediately after that that Irenaeus came from Rome to become bishop of Lyons in place of Pothinus. Irenaeus had already been a presbyter in the diocese of Lyons, and, being highly spoken of, was sent back to carry on the ministry of the church in the immediate wake of the persecution. And it was exactly then that he wrote his *Against the Heresies*, the work which mentions the "Gospel of Judas."

This, I suggest, is the Achilles heel of those who would propose, by whatever means, that we should somehow prefer the gnostic and similar writings to the canonical Scriptures. Reading Ehrman, Meyer and others, it is easy to forget what was really going on at the time, and to imagine that Ignatius, Irenaeus and others like him were simply unpleasant and arrogant heresy-hunters, eager simply to prop up their own power and ecclesiastical systems. That, indeed, is the underlying argument of one of the best-known books within the whole modern rehabilitation of Gnosticism, Elaine Pagels's *The Gnostic Gospels*. Again and again she examines the conflict between emerging orthodoxy and emerging Gnosticism, and offers what she calls a "political" explanation: Ignatius, Irenaeus and the rest were doing what they were doing—including embracing martyrdom, it seems—out of the driving passion they had for political control, for creating a monolithic ecclesial structure.

Nothing could be further from the truth. The people who were being burned at the stake, fried on hot irons, thrown to the wild beasts, pulled apart on the rack, and the other delights which the letter from Vienne and Lyons reports—these people did not imagine themselves to be on the way to a great political victory of "orthodoxy" over "heresy." They were not, as is often suggested, settling down and making comfortable compromises with the status quo, anticipating by over a hundred years the time when, much to the astonishment of the Christians following the horrific persecution of Diocletian, the Christian faith became first permitted and then official. They were following their crucified Lord. If what you want to do is to advance a program for ecclesial structure and control, highlighting your own official position within that program, it hardly seems sensible to embrace and teach a message which is likely to get you and the other key leaders tortured and killed. Rather, what we see in Ignatius and Irenaeus is the natural insistence that, if the authorities are bent on persecuting the church, it is vital that this beleaguered little community stick together, and that it should hold on firmly, not to a grandiose or triumphalistic hierarchical structure, but to that leadership which, precisely by its unity across the traditional dividing lines of the human race, constitutes a sign to the powers of the world that Jesus is Lord and that they are not.[12]

Let's be clear, then. The Christians who died in Gaul in 177, and the thousands who died around the whole Roman Empire in that century, were not reading "Thomas" or "Peter" or the "Gospel of Judas." They were reading, quoting, praying and singing Matthew, Mark, Luke and John—the texts which nurtured their vivid faith in Jesus, not as a revealer of secret truths to help them escape the wicked world, but as the Lord they knew and loved (Irenaeus writes vividly and movingly about this), the one whose death and resurrection had unleashed a new power into the world, into people's lives, giving them hope not for a disembodied spiritual bliss in a non-spatio-temporal world but for the resurrection of the body in the renewal of the created order, a renewal which had already begun and was already making inroads into the real world. They believed in the Jesus who announced God's rule on earth as in heaven, who claimed that all authority not only in heaven (that would have been safe), but on earth as well, had been given to him. The martyrs lived for that vision, and—not surprisingly, since it was and is threatening to many types of political authority—they died for it.

By contrast, why should the gnostic believer worry about standing up and declaring that he or she belonged to the despised company of the Christians? The church, as we have seen, was mocked by the Gnostics for its stance; the "Jesus" of the "Gospel of Judas" laughed at it. Why should one associate with people who went about getting themselves into trouble? And, if the real point of Jesus' teaching was to discover the true divinity within oneself and so escape from the wicked world altogether, why would Caesar persecute a group with that kind of belief? Why would such people feel under any obligation to hold back from giving the pagans the minimal allegiance they required?

This emerges clearly in some of the gnostic texts. Though some within what was admittedly a very diverse movement did attribute value to martyrdom, many others scorned it. Works such as the "Testimony of Truth" and the "Apocalypse of Peter" are emphatic on the matter: the orthodox insistence that martyrdom is a sure way to salvation is mere self-deception.[13] If, as I suggested before, one at least of the roots of second-century Gnosticism was the reaction of some Jews to the disaster of AD 135, we can see why they might think that. The Jews, after all, had clung on to the stories of the Maccabean martyrs from the 160s BC, and had told those stories to sustain their faith in the promises of God that there would come a further and greater revolt against the pagan overlords, and that with that victory the dead would be raised. One can understand that, with the cruel and shocking overthrow of that hope in AD 66–70 and then again in AD 132–35, some who had experienced the latter might turn their back on the whole thing—promises, revolutions, resurrection, martyrdom and all. We should not, in other words, simply reverse the rhetoric of the gnostic writings and pour scorn on their authors as mere cowards. But nor should we be lured into supposing that the proto-orthodox Christians were only interested in social position and their own power systems while it was the Gnostics who represented the really radical and exciting alternative. That bears no relation to the evidence, which is quite clear: as a rule, the Gnostics avoided persecution, while the proto-orthodox, believing still in the Jewish-style vision of God's kingdom confronting that of Caesar, embraced it as a probable consequence of following the crucified Jesus.

Right through the century we see theologians sketching out this picture. Ignatius of Antioch sees that those who say that Christ did not really suffer are also likely to say that martyrdom is unnecessary.[14] Justin, on the way to earning the name of "Martyr," comments that the followers of gnostic teachers such as Simon, Marcion and Valentinus are not persecuted or put to death.[15] Eusebius reports that Basilides, one of the greatest of the gnostic teachers, "taught that there was no harm in eating things offered to idols, or in lightheartedly denying the faith in times of persecution."[16] And Irenaeus describes the clever thought-processes by which the Gnostics were able to avoid persecution:

> As the son was unknown to all, so must they also be known by no one; but while they know all, and pass through all, they themselves remain invisible and unknown to all; for, "You must know all," they say, "but do not let anyone know you." For this reason, persons of such a persuasion are also ready to recant; in fact, it is impossible that they should suffer on account of a mere name, since they are just like all the rest . . . They declare that they are no longer Jews, and that they are not yet Christians; and that it is not at all fitting to speak openly of their mysteries, but right to keep them secret by preserving silence.[17]

In fact, says Irenaeus, some of these people have even poured contempt upon the martyrs, saying it is stupid and ridiculous to follow that path. He allows that some of the Gnostics have indeed been prepared to bear reproach for the name of Christ, but he says that the great majority "maintain that such witness-bearing is not at all necessary, since their system of doctrines is the true witness."[18]

Tertullian, as usual, puts it more dramatically:

> When, therefore, faith is greatly agitated, and the Church burning . . . then the Gnostics break out; then the Valentinians creep forth; then all the opponents of martyrdom bubble up . . . We ourselves, having been appointed for pursuit, are like hares being hemmed in from a distance, while the heretics go about in their normal way . . . They also who oppose martyrdoms, representing salvation to be destruction, turn sweet into bitter, as well as light into darkness.[19]

Various writers have commented on the way in which the Gnostics resisted martyrdom or avoided it altogether. The point itself is uncontroversial. But it regularly goes unnoticed in contemporary discussion of different kinds of gospels and so forth. The facts of second-century persecution and martyrdom are telling, and they give the lie in particular to the regular charge that the "orthodox" were simply in the business of political power and control while the "heretics" were the ones at risk. It certainly didn't look like that to the Christians, or indeed to the pagans, of Vienne or Lyons. If for the first time in the modern period we are reading a text which up to now we knew almost exclusively through a work written by the Bishop of Lyons in about 180, we should pay careful attention to the context within which the Bishop of Lyons was writing, not least the fact that he had just succeeded the previous bishop who had died for the same faith. We would do well to ponder the different stances we have now sketched, and the outcome of their very different belief systems.

I wrote the first draft of those last paragraphs on Holy Saturday, 2006. The next day, one of the leading Patristic scholars of our time, the Archbishop of Canterbury, Dr. Rowan Williams, said this in his Easter sermon in Canterbury Cathedral:

> [The New Testament] was written by people who, by writing what they did and believing what they did, were making themselves, in the world's terms, less powerful, not more. They were walking out into an unmapped territory, away from the safe places of political and religious influence, away from traditional Jewish religion and from Roman society and law. As the gospels and Paul's letters . . . all agree, they were putting themselves in a place where they shared the humiliation experienced by condemned criminals going naked in public procession to their execution.[20]

And what was true for the earliest Christians, and the writers of the New Testament, was graphically and demonstrably true for people like Ignatius, Polycarp, Justin and Irenaeus in the second century. They were the ones who were going out into the unknown, away from safety. Here is the irony: that the gnostic gospels are today being trumpeted as the radical alternatives to the oppressive and conservative canonical gospels, but the historical reality was just the opposite. The Gnostics were quite content to capitulate to their surrounding culture, in which mystery-religions, self-discovery, Platonic spirituality of various sorts, and coded revelations of hidden truths were the stock in trade. In other words, the Gnostics were the cultural conservatives, sticking with the kind of religion that everyone already knew. As such, when we read their writings without the rose-tinted spectacles of Meyer, Ehrman and others, they are bound to strike us (to use our modern, anachronistic language) as fairly thoroughly sexist, anti-Semitic, and lacking the courage to stand out against the ideologies and authorities of their day. It was the orthodox Christians who were breaking new ground, and risking their necks as they did so.

Those who were prepared to die for their loyalty to Jesus, and for their belief in the achievement of his death and resurrection, were therefore embracing a "salvation" which meant something quite different from what "salvation" and similar language means in the "Gospel of Judas" and cognate writings. This is so in terms both of the *goal* and the *means* of salvation.

The goal of salvation, in the New Testament and the early Fathers, is the remaking of the good, God-given created universe, and the resurrection of the body for those who have died, so that they can share in the world that has been put to rights. "Salvation" means rescue from that which defaces and corrupts God's good creation, i.e. death and all that leads toward it. As I have argued in detail elsewhere, for the early Christians, as for the early rabbis, three things go together: a belief in the essential goodness of creation, a belief in the ultimate justice of God (i.e. a belief that God the creator will one day put everything to rights), and a belief, exactly correlated with the other two, in the coming resurrection of the body as part of the coming restoration of all things.[21] What Gnosticism offers is not a variation on this, not another way of looking at or expressing substantially the same point, but a view of salvation which flatly contradicts this early Christian (and early Jewish) view at every point. For Gnosticism, the created order is essentially bad. There is no point in expecting things to be put right within it either now or in the future. Salvation therefore consists precisely not in resurrection—why would you want to get a body back again?—but in escaping from it altogether. As Bart Ehrman expresses it graphically,

> According to most gnostics, this material world is *not* our home. We are trapped here, in these bodies of flesh, and we need to learn how to escape . . . Since the point is to allow the soul to leave this world behind and to enter into "that great and holy generation"—that is, the divine realm that transcends this world—a resurrection of the body is the very last thing that Jesus, or any of his true followers, would want.[22]

And if the ultimate goal is utterly different for the New Testament on the one hand and the gnostic literature on the other, the way to that goal is, not surprisingly, different as well. For the earliest Christians, and for the great teachers of the second century like Polycarp, Justin and Irenaeus, the way to the ultimate life, to the resurrection itself, was Jesus himself: not the Jesus of the gnostic imagination or reconstruction, but the Jesus who announced and embodied God's kingdom as it was arriving on earth as in heaven, the Jesus who went to his death not to escape this material world but to rescue it, the Jesus who rose again to launch God's project of new creation and to rule over God's whole creation as its rightful Lord. And, according to the earliest Christians, the way this Jesus rescues people and remakes them in the present time so that they already share in this new world, and look forward to its completion hereafter, is through the word of the gospel, which works in people's hearts and minds by the Spirit; through the faith which believes that word and comes to know the living presence of Jesus and submit to his Lordship; through baptism, which incorporates people into the dying and rising of Jesus and hence into the company of those who belong to him; through holiness of life, which works out the meaning of new creation in hard physical reality; and, if one is so called, through martyrdom, which embraces the same end as Jesus had suffered, in order that, like the brigand on the cross, the martyr might be with Jesus in Paradise and eventually share in the resurrection itself.

For the Gnostic, again, none of this is relevant. The way to salvation—the alternative "salvation" of escaping this world—is through *knowledge*, knowledge of the secrets about the world and about one's true self. Ehrman again:

> For gnostics, a person is saved not by having faith in Christ or by doing good works [Ehrman is here confusing Paul's teaching about "salvation" with his view of "justification," but this need not distract us here]. Rather, a person is saved by knowing the truth—the truth about the world we live in, about who the true God is, and especially about who we ourselves are. In other words, this is largely self-knowledge: Knowledge of where we came from, how we got here, and how we can return to our heavenly home . . . For those gnostics

who were also Christian (many gnostics were not), it is
Christ himself who brings this secret knowledge from
above. He reveals the truth to his intimate followers,
and it is this truth that can set them free.[23]

It is not simply, in other words, the nature of salvation,
and the way to attain it, that has been transformed
within Gnosticism. It is the figure of "Jesus" or "Christ"
as well. Though Ehrman here uses Johannine language
("you shall know the truth, and the truth shall set you
free"[24]), the "truth" which the Gnostic supposes has
been revealed by this "Jesus" is very different from
that on offer within the canonical gospels and the other
earliest Christian writings.

At the center of the whole picture we find the question: is "salvation" an act of undeserved divine *love* and
grace, reaching out to those who had nothing to commend them, as Paul and John so dramatically put it?
Or is it an act of revelation, and of discovery *of what is
already there*, with the "revealer" revealing what is already true about a person, and the person in question
discovering who he or she truly is? Is "salvation," after
all, simply a matter of discovering your own "star" and
following it? That is the all-important difference, in
terms of "salvation," between the early and historically
rooted Christian faith and the gnostic proposal. And
that highlights the question: what is going on in the
present time when scholars and popularizers not only

make texts like the "Gospel of Judas" freshly available, for which all of us who are interested in the ancient world are profoundly grateful, but also urge it upon us, commending it as a new and exciting angle on Jesus and Christianity?

Part of the answer, to be sure, lies in the publishers' desire to make money. Which would you prefer: to publish the text in an academic monograph which will sell a few thousand copies to libraries and scholars, or to set it out in a racy, now-at-last-we-know-the-truth presentation which will hit the bestseller lists? But the scholars who are involved with the project are not simply Dan Browns with PhDs. They assuredly know what they are doing, and what they are commending. What are they really trying to tell us, and how should we respond?

6

Spinning Judas:
The New Myth of Christian Origins

One of the first things that the editors of the "Gospel of Judas" have tried to make out—and one of the things that have inevitably attracted headlines—is that this new document rehabilitates Judas Iscariot, after all the bad press he has had for betraying Jesus to the authorities. Marvin Meyer waxes eloquent on the subject:

> In contrast to the New Testament gospels, Judas Iscariot is presented as a thoroughly positive figure in the Gospel of Judas, a role model for all those who wish to be disciples of Jesus . . . The point of the gospel is the insight

and loyalty of Judas as the paradigm of discipleship. In the end, he does exactly what Jesus wants.[1]

Well, yes, he does; but what this "Jesus" wants, and the reason he wants it, are, as Meyer explains carefully elsewhere, completely different from anything we can imagine of the Jesus of Matthew, Mark, Luke and John. Meyer continues, painting a dark backcloth against which the jewel of this new discovery will shine the more brightly:

> In the biblical tradition, however, Judas—whose name has been linked to "Jew" and "Judaism"—was often portrayed as the evil Jew who turned Jesus in to be arrested and killed, and thereby the biblical figure of Judas the Betrayer has fed the flames of anti-Semitism. Judas in the present gospel may counteract this anti-Semitic tendency. He does nothing Jesus himself does not ask him to do, and he listens to Jesus and remains faithful to him. In the Gospel of Judas, Judas Iscariot turns out to be Jesus' beloved disciple and dear friend.[2]

Notice how Meyer smuggles in a medieval view into the canonical gospels in order to make it appear that the "Gospel of Judas" presents a good, and politically correct, answer to them. Nowhere in Matthew, Mark, Luke or John is there in fact the slightest suggestion that Judas's betrayal, and his guilt for it, have anything whatever to do with his being a *Jew*. When Meyer says "the biblical tradition," he really means "the tradition which, a thousand years after the Bible was written, used it in one particular way." As we have said already, Jesus was a Jew; all the disciples were Jewish; two other people in Jesus' immediate following (one of the Twelve, and one of Jesus' own brothers) were called "Judah."

But what Meyer never tells us at this point, because though he knows it well enough he also knows that it would blow this whole rehabilitation-of-Judas idea out of the water, is that the entire worldview of Gnosticism, to which the "Gospel of Judas" makes such an interesting fresh contribution, is inherently opposed to the fundamental worldview of mainline Judaism itself. Judaism, from Genesis to the rabbis and beyond, believes in the goodness of the created world, and in the special calling of Israel to be the light of that world. Gnosticism believes in the fundamental badness of the created world, the folly of those who take the Old Testament as their guide, and the special status of the Gnostics as the sparks of light who are to be rescued from that world. In particular, Judaism believes that the God of Israel is the good, wise and sovereign creator of all that is, while Gnosticism believes that the God of Israel is the incompetent and malicious demiurge who made this wicked world. If Gnosticism is true, Judaism is not, and vice versa.

Perhaps because he sees that retort coming, Meyer tries to make out that the "Gospel of Judas" is in fact using some "Jewish" ideas. But of course they are "Jewish gnostic" ones:

> Additionally, the mysteries he learns from Jesus are steeped in Jewish gnostic lore, and the teacher of these mysteries, Jesus, is the master, the rabbi. The Christian Gospel of Judas is at peace with a Jewish view—an alternative Jewish view, to be sure—of gnostic thought, and Jewish gnostic thought has been baptized in Christian gnostic thought.[3]

The best one can say of this is that it is wishful thinking. It may well be, as some leading experts suppose, and as I explored in chapter 2 above, that the second-century Gnosticism we find in Nag Hammadi, the "Gospel of Judas" and elsewhere does indeed have some specifically Jewish roots: why else would such a blatantly Hellenistic movement, so soaked in Platonism, make continual reference to Jewish Scriptures and do so much to reinterpret them and to fit them into its preferred worldview? The social circumstances created a plausible context, as I suggested (the failure of hope after the Bar-Kochba revolt); the philosophical climate was favorable (Philo, a century before, had produced a brilliant synthesis of traditional Jewish belief and Platonic philosophy, though Philo never articulated anything like Gnosticism). What may well have happened is that some Jewish thinkers and mystics in the first two centuries, parallel in some ways to Philo but going way beyond him, and expressing their anger and disappointment with the failure of their own traditional faith and hope, began to offer a form of religion which kept some of the outward symbols or stories of ancient Judaism but which replaced its inner core, particularly its belief in the one God as the good and wise creator, with its polar opposite.[4] The only really "Jewish" thing about the "Gospel of Judas" is that, by referring to Adam, Seth and so on, it makes use of the book of Genesis. But it does so in order to subvert Judaism, to overturn it completely from within, by deliberately reading the text against the grain. If "Judas" was written by the "Cainites," they were deliberately making the villain of Genesis (Cain) into the hero, just as they were doing to the apparent villain (Judas) of the gospels. Such a reading "makes use of" Genesis in much the same way as a child might "use" a Shakespeare play by tearing out a page to make a paper dart.

Bart Ehrman also attempts to "rehabilitate" Judas. Having already declared that Judas, in this new "Gospel," is "the consummate insider, the one to whom Jesus delivers his secret revelation," he suggests that this should alter the Christian view of Judaism:

> If Judas didn't betray Jesus, then that would change
> how Christians understood their relationship, not only

to the betrayer but also to the people whom the betrayer is thought to represent, mainly ["namely"?] the Jews. So, throughout the course of Christian history, Christians have blamed the Jews for the death of Jesus and Judas is emblematic of the Jew who betrayed Jesus. If in fact Jesus and Judas were in agreement about Judas's mission, that would change the understanding of the relationship of Jews and Christians.[5]

To which, of course, we must respond that if this supposed "agreement" about Judas's mission was an agreement on a worldview and theology which ran in the diametrically opposite direction to that of most first-century Jews (apart, at best, from a few hypothetical groups who had already abandoned any belief in the goodness of creation, and who have left no evidence to speak of), then it might indeed change the understanding of the relationship of Jews and Christians—by showing that genuine Judaism and genuine Christianity have a good deal more in common with one another than either of them do with the worldview represented by the "Gospel of Judas"! But Ehrman digs himself in deeper still:

> If it turns out that Judas didn't betray Jesus, but simply did what Jesus wanted him to do, then this would show that Jesus was a continuation of Judaism rather than somebody who is representing a break with Judaism. And if historically Jesus didn't represent a break with

Judaism, then that would have a significant impact on the relationship of Jews and Christians today, because these wouldn't represent historically two different religions, these would represent the same religion.[6]

This, again, may be wishful thinking, but it also represents a fearful muddle. Nobody in the first century—certainly not the canonical evangelists or their sources—saw the betrayal of Judas as in any sense a sign of a "break" between Jesus and Judaism. Like Meyer, Ehrman is simply reading medieval ideas back into texts which are completely innocent of them. The question of the relationship between the Jesus movement and first-century Judaism is indeed a complicated one, and does indeed have all kinds of ramifications in our own day. But any suggestion that a revisionist account of Judas and his betrayal will throw the switch between a "Jesus against Judaism" view and a "Jesus within Judaism" view is whistling in the wind. Once again, everything we know about Jesus and the first Christians on the one hand, and everything we know about the main lines of Judaism in the first century—the Pharisees, the Essenes, the author of the Wisdom of Solomon, Josephus, even the Platonizer Philo—suggests that they had a great deal more in common with one another than with Gnosticism, particularly the sort of Gnosticism we see in the "Gospel of Judas."

We must not forget (though Meyer and Ehrman conveniently seem to forget it when proposing this "rehabilitation" of Judas as striking a significant blow for Jewish-Christian relationships) that the "Gospel of Judas" speaks of the creator God, the God of Judaism, as an inferior and actually malevolent deity. As Ehrman says elsewhere (and as we could have deduced quite easily from other documents like the "Gospel of Thomas"), for the Gnostics this Jewish god is not to be worshiped but to be avoided.[7] For the loyal Jew, from that day to this, the fundamental confession of faith is, "Hear, O Israel: YHWH our God, YHWH is one."[8] Anyone praying that prayer three times a day would know perfectly well that to embrace the worldview offered by the "Gospel of Judas" would mean not just a break, a discontinuity, but a deep and radical disloyalty, an overturning of the most basic Jewish conviction. We might note the comment of a leading contemporary Jewish scholar, Guy Stroumsa:

> The Gnostics' attitude towards the God of Israel as an inferior deity and the Prophets of Israel as his minions is a clear example of what can be called metaphysical anti-Semitism.[9]

In similar vein, a leading Jewish scholar of Christian origins, Professor Amy-Jill Levine of Vanderbilt Divinity School, writes:

Not only will this revised version of Judas have no impact on Jewish-Christian relations, the Gospel of Judas proclaims a theology that is not good for the Jews, and not good for the Christians either . . . I'd prefer to keep the God of Israel rather than have Judas as a hero; I'd prefer to keep the Law and the Prophets rather than learn about enlightened aeons, and I'd prefer to honor the body rather than to cast it off.[10]

All this does somewhat undermine the touching belief of Frieda Tchacos Nussberger (who negotiated the eventual purchase and hence the editing of the text) that she had been "predestined by Judas to rehabilitate him."[11] And the repetition by Krosney of the suggestion by Meyer and Ehrman, that this new "Gospel" will eliminate the medieval notion of collective guilt ("the Gospel of Judas offers no blood libel that will course through history, causing vilification of Jews, pogroms, and even the Holocaust"), makes clear what is going on.[12] As so often in the ethical wasteland of postmodernity, the shadow of the Holocaust is invoked as a now rather tired way of claiming high moral ground. But just because the "Judas" of this document "obeys his beloved master's wishes," as Krosney puts it, that is no reason to suppose that this will make residual anti-Semites come to their senses. After all, the document says nothing about Judas being Jewish; and all that it does say about the Jewish people, by strong implication, is that they are worshipping the wrong deity. They are to be laughed at, and their worldview is to be rejected.

But it isn't only a rehabilitation of Judas that the editors claim is on offer in this text. It is also a new and inspiring vision of Jesus himself. This seems clearly to be what Meyer has in mind in describing the message of the text as "good news":

> The message of the Gospel of Judas is that, just as Jesus is a spiritual being who has come from above and will return to glory, so also the true followers of Jesus are people of soul, whose being and destiny are with the divine . . . at the end of their mortal lives, people who belong to that great generation of Seth will abandon everything of this mortal world, in order to free the inner person and liberate the soul . . . Jesus proclaims a mystical message of hope and freedom.[13]

Hope and freedom maybe, but not in any sense that the earliest Christians would have understood.

Does the text, then, as Ehrman claims, "open up new vistas for understanding Jesus and the religious movement he founded"?[14] Not in the sense that he intends. Yes: it does shed some new light—not very much, but a bit—on the second-century gnostic teachings about which we already knew quite a lot and which here acquire some new and fascinating twists. No, in that it tells us nothing about Jesus of Nazareth; only about some ways in which his name was subsequently used to legitimize teachings utterly foreign to his announcement of God's kingdom on earth as in heaven. The "Gospel of Judas" is indeed "fresh and authentic" in the sense that it is a newly discovered and edited manuscript giving us access to a genuinely early document from the second century. But it has nothing "fresh" or "authentic" to say about Jesus himself and his earliest followers.[15]

On the contrary. Despite the protestations of Meyer, Ehrman, Pagels and others quoted by Krosney, the "Gospel of Judas" is, line by line, a flat and thorough denial of what the canonical gospels are saying.[16] Krosney himself, summarizing the teaching of the book, gives the game away fairly conclusively:

> [The document] was believed by certain people who genuinely regarded Jesus as the true messiah because of the shining example he set and because he could lead each person to the god inside himself or herself . . . Jesus is not a tormented figure who will die in agony on the cross. Instead, he is friendly and benevolent teacher with a sense of humor.[17]

No one who understood the canonical gospels could imagine that this was anything other than the cancellation of their entire theology and the substitution of a different one altogether. And no one who understood the real meaning of Jesus' laughter in this new text would suppose it marked Jesus out as "friendly and benevolent."[18] If it is benevolence we are looking for, we will find it, not in the "Gospel of Judas," but in the New Testament. The figure on the cross may be "tormented," but the reason is clear: "The son of God loved me and gave himself for me."[19]

So why have Meyer, Ehrman and others been so eager to make out that the "Gospel of Judas" is exciting and important not just for our understanding of early Christianity but for today? Why do they suggest that it contains such vital new insights? The answer is that their energetic propagation of the work is part of a larger story, a story which many in our day, particularly in North America, are eager to teach and believe, even at the cost of writing what most historians will regard as manifest nonsense. This is what I call the New Myth of Christian Origins.[20]

The main lines of the new Myth are clear—and Bart Ehrman is currently one of the best known of its current scholarly proponents.[21] There is no space here for a full exposition and comment, but it is vital that we understand the shape and thrust of this movement, and see why an eagerness to propagate it has led Ehrman and others into such enthusiasm for the "Gospel of Judas."

First, according to the new Myth, Jesus was not like the canonical gospels portray him. He did not see himself as in any way divine. He did not intend to die for the sins of the world. He certainly did not rise again from the dead. Rather, Jesus was a teacher of strange and subversive wisdom, who generated a pluriform tradition in which many movements sprang up, writing and editing many versions of his life, his sayings, and his fate.

Second, there were a great many different varieties of early Christianity, and they produced a large number of different "gospels," all of which circulated in early Christian circles more or less unchecked. It was only after the Constantinian settlement in the early fourth century that the church decided to highlight Matthew, Mark, Luke and John and to reject all the others. And the reason for this choice, it is suggested again and again by proponents of the new Myth, is because the church was interested all along in political power and control, and so was eager to prioritize books that would provide it—not least by speaking of a divine Jesus instead of the human one found in the other gospels.[22]

Third, the teaching that was thus rejected was not at all about the Jewish and early Christian vision of the kingdom of the creator God coming on earth as in heaven. It was about seeking true meaning inside oneself—and, more than true meaning, true goodness and even true divinity. It had nothing to do with the need for an atonement; humans, at least the special ones, were not sinners in need of forgiveness, but sparks of light who needed to discover who they were. It had nothing whatever to do with the dream, let alone the reality, of resurrection. It offered a different kind of religion, more like a soft version of Buddhism . . .

. . . and more in tune with the hopes of liberal American academics from the 1960s onwards, especially those who had grown up in somewhat strict versions of the Christian faith, whether traditional Catholic or traditional (and perhaps fundamentalist) Protestant. Krosney, perhaps naively, quotes a telling passage from the classicist Roger Bagnall, which those who know the field will recognize as dead-on accurate:

> If you think about the state of religious studies as an academic discipline in the 1960s and 1970s [he is referring to North America], you will recognize that it was heavily populated with people who came out of theological backgrounds, often deep church backgrounds, and who had a highly conflicted attitude toward that part of their background. [That is academic-speak for saying, "and had firmly rejected what they were taught in Sunday school."] The Nag Hammadi material was of course heretical in a technical sense, stuff condemned by the orthodox fathers of the church. A scholar who had no personal stake in Christianity would be unlikely to feel a need to come to terms with that, but this was hardly the case. If you read Elaine Pagels, you'll see the result: The Gnostics are validated as a direction in

which Christianity could have gone and which would have made it warmer and fuzzier, much nicer than this cold orthodoxy stuff.[23]

It is refreshing to hear the truth spoken like that—though depressing to think of the vision of "orthodoxy" which would have made it appear cold and oppressive compared with the radical dualism, the hatred for the world, of the Gnostics. The reference to Elaine Pagels, whose work we have already mentioned in various contexts, is telling: in her famous book *The Gnostic Gospels* she continually draws parallels between facets of ancient gnostic belief and telltale aspects of our contemporary self-help culture such as (some forms of) Buddhism, existentialism and the psychotherapy movement.[24] At one point she likens Gnosticism to the philosophy of Feuerbach, a nineteenth-century German whose proposal, that when we talk about God we are really talking about humankind, was important for the existentialist theology of the 1930s, and for the revisionist theories which grew from that, providing the soil in which the new Myth has grown and flourished.[25] Anything will do, it seems, as long as it is not classic Judaism or Christianity.

This contemporary North American movement is somewhat selective in its favoring of Gnosticism, but I shall return to that in a moment. The point is that the fashion for favoring gnostic texts, even admittedly very bizarre ones, over against the canonical Scriptures has a great deal more to do with social and religious (or indeed anti-religious) fashions in North America than with actual historical research. Of course there are major and serious historical issues to be faced. But the power of the Myth—as revealed in the media firestorm every time another scrap of "evidence" turns up which can be "spun" so as to favor the Myth rather than mainline Christianity—is such that these are swept up in the onward rush to believe what the Myth demands.

In particular, then, the new Myth wants us to believe that if we want genuine, liberating religion we shall find it in the gnostic vision rather than the mainline Christian one. Here once more is Marvin Meyer:

> In the Gospel of Truth [a well known gnostic tractate found in Nag Hammadi] the fruit of knowledge is a discovery bringing joy. It signifies that one finds god in oneself, that the fog of error and terror is gone, and that the nightmare of darkness is exchanged for an eternal heavenly day.[26]

This is hardly a dispassionate statement of a viewpoint from which one wishes to distance oneself. And the viewpoint in question is one which, as well as being favorable to the new Myth of Christian Origins, belongs in a larger and still more powerful cultural matrix: that of the Protestant churches, especially the North American Protestant churches, over the last two hundred years.

This is perhaps the most disturbing thing to emerge as we study the "Gospel of Judas" and reflect on why it has been "spun" in the way it has.

In the autumn of 1982 I was teaching at McGill University in Montreal, Canada. Over lunch one day I met a visiting scholar who talked to me about his research project. We never met again, but over the succeeding years, though my research took me in different directions from his, I often wondered how he had got on. Finally, quite recently, I bought and read his book. I wish I had done so earlier.

The scholar in question is Philip J. Lee, a Presbyterian minister from New Brunswick, Canada. His thesis, which has received some enthusiastic reviews from theologians and cultural critics alike, is that a kind of Gnosticism has been deeply entrenched in North American Protestant Christianity, and that it has generated all kinds of ills not only in the church but in the wider society. His book, *Against the Protestant Gnostics*, is a polemic whose time has, I believe, more than fully come.[27]

Lee categorizes the typical American religion as elitist: it favors the self-knowing individual over the believing community. It has regularly opted for what he calls "selective syncretism" over against the particularity of actual religious traditions. It is both escapist, withdrawing from the world of politics and society, and narcissistic, seeking its own identity and fulfilment. In its rejection of the goodness of creation, it has invited Americans to think of the natural world simply as a place to exploit, opening up the imagination to embrace ecological carelessness and wanton violence—which, as Lee points out in the preface to the paperback edition, has been an increasingly disturbing feature of American public life.

This is not the place to go into Lee's analysis in detail, or to engage in the wider cultural discussion which his book prompts. He seems to me considerably to over-state his case, as groundbreaking polemicists often do. His attempts to sketch a lengthy genealogy of modern Gnosticism, tracing it all the way back to elements in the Calvinism of the Founding Fathers, strike me sometimes as far-fetched. His work needs balancing and modifying by others, not least by more subtle works such as that of Cyril O'Regan.[28] But this brief mention serves to set in its larger context both the new "Myth" of which I have spoken and the enthusiasm for (some features at least of) ancient Gnosticism which it generates and sustains.

In particular, Western Protestantism since the Enlightenment, and perhaps before, has fostered the possibility of conspiracy theories. The church, the "establishment," or whoever, has been interested in its own power and prestige, and thus has suppressed the "real truth" about its own historical origins—and, with that, the "real religion" that Jesus is supposed to have taught and exemplified. For serious thinkers in the eighteenth and nineteenth centuries, this question had a thoroughly positive side, jolting the church out of complacency and forcing it to do some serious historical work. But in the debased form such conspiracy theories have taken in recent years, the Protestant instinct to question previous "certainties" has been downgraded further into the postmodern instinct to disbelieve everything. As Rowan Williams says, in the sermon already quoted:

> We are instantly fascinated by the suggestion of conspiracies and cover-ups; this has become so much the stuff of our imagination these days that it is only natural, it seems, to expect it when we turn to ancient texts, especially biblical texts. We treat them as if they were unconvincing press releases from some official source, whose intention is to conceal the real story; and that real story waits for the intrepid investigator to uncover it and share it with the waiting world. Anything that looks like the official version is automatically suspect. Someone is trying to stop you finding out what really happened, because what really happened could upset or challenge the power of officialdom. It all makes a good and characteristically "modern" story—about resisting authority, bringing secrets to light, exposing corruption and deception; it evokes Watergate and *All the President's Men*.[29]

Just so. But this relentless hermeneutic of suspicion does not result in a kind of equilibrium, leaving us without any ruling theories or dominant religious proposals and impulses. Rather—Lee's point is that this represents the whole underlying trend of American Protestantism—it strongly favors forms of Gnosticism, especially the idea that "discovering who I really am" is the primary religious imperative, since "who I really am" is in fact some kind of a divine being. Lee quotes Tom Wolfe to powerful effect, pointing out that, among other features, the sexual revolution has been justified in almost religious terms: the divine spark at the apex of my soul (which is, after all, how the sexual impulse often presents itself) must come to its fruition, at whatever cost in terms of breaking links with the past and the future, with family and friends.[30]

That is why, within the church life and theology which has embraced this new and at least quasi-gnostic account of Christian origins and Christian faith, the primary source of "authority" is one's own *experience*. If the point of the religious quest is to discover the divine spark within one's own self, to pay attention to that inner experience will—must!—trump any appeal to any other supposed source of authority. Indeed, as we have seen, part of the whole point of the gnostic movement was to cut loose from external authority and follow one's own star. Even if this led to solitude—one might almost say, solipsism—it was vital to go with "the primacy of immediate experience."[31] This is what lies at the root of some of the critical debates in the church today: when people speak of an "appeal to experience" or the need to "listen to experience," some at least intend those phrases to be heard within a worldview where "experience" is, by definition, the ultimate authority, since one's inner "experience" is the clue to one's secret inner divine nature, now at last revealed. On the day I was editing this book for publication, I happened to be in Toronto, and saw, outside a popular midtown church, a saying of Carl Jung: "Who looks outside, dreams; who looks inside, awakens." Modern Gnosticism in a nutshell.

But of course the contemporary appeal to Gnosticism is selective. Some of the early Gnostics took their dualism to imply a commitment to a serious asceticism. They really did cut their ties with the world of space, time and matter. They really did renounce all sensual pleasures and earthly prospects. There is—how can one say this without sounding cynical oneself?—not much evidence that contemporary American Gnosticism is taking this route. Rather, it attempts to have the best of both worlds. First, a "quest for the divine" which turns out to be the quest for self-discovery, leading to a religiously propagated existentialism in which "discovering who I am," as the primal obligation, leads to the secondary obligation of "being true to who I am"—even if that means being false to all sorts of other things. Second, a relentless and culturally mandated "pursuit of happiness" in terms of the kind of material and emotional well-being which would have appalled the hard-line ancient Gnostic. That's quite a combination.

Most people do not, of course, think it through like that. For some, the implicit rhetoric of the first, more "spiritual," agenda may actually become implicitly coalesced with the second, more "material" agenda. For others, the gnostic imperative can easily join with the Enlightenment's insistence on the absolute separation of church and state, of religion and politics. We live in the "upstairs" world in our religious lives, and then we get on with our "downstairs" lives of making money, chasing after happiness, and so on, without any sense of incongruity. Indeed, Gnosticism insisted, as we have seen, precisely on that split between religion and earthly reality which the Enlightenment insisted on, for quite other reasons to be sure but with a fascinating and powerful convergence of cultural impulses.

A further telling sign emerges at this point. The radical dualism embodied in the "Gospel of Judas" has a good deal in common with the equally radical dualism embodied in the dispensationalist fundamentalism so popular in many parts of North America, and now expressed famously in the Left Behind novels. The main aim in both, after all, is to escape from this wicked world and go off to a different one, namely "heaven," rather than (with the New Testament) to seek for God's kingdom to come on earth as in heaven.[32] I doubt if Ehrman and Meyer will take kindly to the suggestion that they are second cousins of the dualistic fundamentalism represented by that movement, but the evidence is clear. "This world is not my home; I'm just a-passing through." So sing the fundamentalists; but the Gnostics would have agreed.

When applied in right-wing terms, this selective neo-Gnosticism can justify everything from the so-called "prosperity gospel" (if I am a faithful Christian, God will make me rich; I belong, after all, to his elite) to the idea that the American people possess a "manifest destiny" to bring order to the rest of the world. The point is this: if we are the "enlightened" ones, leaving behind the constraints of earlier superstition and ignorance, then we have not just the chance but actually the duty to behave as befits the elite of the world, including where necessary inflicting on others the appropriate punishment for their persistent blindness, their failure to see what we see.[33] Who can deny that there is at least an element of this in some of the attitudes adopted by some European leaders over the last two hundred years, and some American ones more recently?

When applied in left-wing terms, selective neo-Gnosticism can justify everything from blatant syncretism on the religious front to complete disregard for classic sexual moral norms. After all (with regard to the first), if Jesus is simply the one who reveals to us the divinity that lies within us, then there may be other revealers, too; and if the point of Christianity is not the rescue operation whereby the world's creator sends his son to die and rise to redeem the world, but the revelation of a divinity already present within us (well, some of us at least), then we have distanced ourselves from what most Christians since the first century have believed, and brought ourselves a good deal closer to what all kinds of other religious movements have believed.

And, with regard to the second, if my innermost "experience" is the ultimate test of religious or spiritual validity, and my innermost "identity" is the ultimate goal of my religious or spiritual quest, then discovering my own sexual identity, and giving it full expression, takes precedence over the restrictive and externally applied moral codes culled from ancient texts which may, after all, have less validity than we used to think.[34] Who can deny that there are elements of these impulses in much contemporary discourse, both inside the churches and outside?

Underneath both right and left, it is all the same religious belief, far more in tune with ancient Gnosticism than with classic Christianity: what matters is not the outward world, the wider community, or even the outward physical human being, but the supposed spark of true "identity" that lies within the individual. At the corporate level, one cannot but notice the way in which the storyline mirrors the classic narrative of American liberation (and I am fully aware of the irony of this point being made by me, as an English bishop): in the late eighteenth century, precisely when the "Enlightenment" was at its height, the nascent United States declared that it was discovering its own identity and that it was not going to dance to the tunes played by King George III and . . . the bishops he was sending to the colonies! That may well have been good politics and statesmanship. I hold no brief for the bizarre things my ancestors got up to. But it is hardly a secure narrative foundation on which to build a religious or spiritual worldview.

And, at the individual level, we are not surprised when Herbert Krosney summarizes the teaching of the "Gospel of Judas," and its relevance for today, in terms which I have quoted already but which bear repetition since they fit Lee's thesis like a glove:

> Following our own star is an idea that is as relevant today as it was back then. Rather than cast out the betrayer, perhaps we should look more deeply for the goodness inside ourselves.[35]

The question which remains, though, is: how credible is all this? Has the "Gospel of Judas" perhaps betrayed the secret of modern Gnosticism? Might the publication of this very explicit statement of second-century Gnosticism be the point at which the movement represented by Meyer, Ehrman, Pagels and others has overreached itself, has overplayed its hand?

7

THE CHALLENGE OF "JUDAS" FOR TODAY

In this final chapter I want to suggest, as I have just hinted, that the "Gospel of Judas" might indeed represent the point at which the ordinary reader, long used to being fed a diet of conspiracy theories, "secret gospels," "lost sources," and a host of similar things, would at last wake up, rub her eyes, and declare that if *that's* what it's all about—meaning by "that" the kind of thing we find in "Judas"—then it's obviously all a mistake, and maybe there is something in classic Christianity after all. Whatever we think about the historical Judas Iscariot and his "betrayal" of Jesus, perhaps this "Gospel of Judas" has betrayed at last the secret which the gnostic enthusiasts have kept under wraps in their efforts to persuade us that the Nag Hammadi texts and other similar documents were after all superior in religious quality, as well as in date, to the canonical gospels. When we look at "Judas" we see what we are really up against.

Despite the fact that Meyer, Ehrman and others do their best to persuade us that the worldview represented by "Judas" has a lot to commend it, I sense that at some points they know they are struggling. It isn't just that they have to apologize, as we saw earlier, for the wonderfully rambling and obscure cosmology. No: it is that the worldview of "Judas" is so dark, so uncompromising, so utterly dualistic, that they must know that the ordinary reader, not least in cheerfully affluent North America, is very unlikely to take it seriously. The only thing to hope for, it seems, is bodily death: is that really a message likely to appeal even to the gnostically inclined in today's world? Or, if it is (we cannot but be reminded of the Heaven's Gate suicides and other similar phenomena), is it the sort of thing that the enthusiastic supporters of the "Gospel of Judas" intend to encourage?

In particular, we cannot help noticing that, just as "Judas" thinks that the world of space, time and matter is a dark and wicked place, so there is no promise that it will ever be anything else. Along with creation, Israel, atonement and resurrection, another Jewish and Christian doctrine that "Judas" leaves out of the equation, because it would make no sense in that worldview, is judgment. Just in case anyone reacts to the word "judgment" by saying, "There! That's what I was brought up on—all that hellfire and damnation; and that's what I have thankfully abandoned," we should remind ourselves that in the biblical tradition judgment is emphatically *good* news, not bad. It means that the creator God has promised to make the world right at last, to sort it out, to sift it and straighten it and heal its ancient wounds and wrongs. It is, in particular, good news for the poor and the oppressed. God's kingdom will come, and his will be done, on earth as in heaven; indeed, heaven and earth will at the last be united. That is the promise of the New Testament, building firmly on ancient Jewish roots and seeing them come into fresh focus through Jesus and his death and resurrection.[1]

And "Judas" will have none of it. The "Jesus" of this new "Gospel" laughs at people who think that way, and worship that kind of god. He offers a different message: the present world is a snare and a delusion, and you shouldn't be bothering about it. Those who live by "Judas" and similar works can sidestep the clash with the principalities and powers of this world, in which the Christians of the second and third centuries—the time when Gnosticism was at its height in the penumbra of the ancient Christian community—were being persecuted with sporadic ferocity. There may well be

139

cultural reasons in today's world to explain how many people feel alienated within our contemporary society, and so are naturally drawn to Gnosticism, in parallel with those who first propagated it. But the fact that some people find the world such a threatening and gloomy place that they naturally incline to radical dualism, while it may help to explain the rise of the suicide rate in many parts of the Western world, is hardly an argument for saying that they should be encouraged to wallow in that condition, still less to imagine that this is what Jesus came to teach.

So what is really going on with the new "Myth of Christian Origins," and with the larger gnosticizing tendency within American Protestantism, and, more specifically, the attempt to propose the adopting of Gnosticism as the appropriate alternative to classic Christianity? Many things, no doubt, but one of them is this. Once you have removed "religion" from the real world, there is no imperative to *do* anything about that world. Take away the notion of the world as the good creation of the good God, and the belief that this god intends to put the world to rights at last, and you cut the nerve of the imperative to anticipate that final justice by working for it, in advance, in the present time. All you are left with (along with the need to escape by "discovering who you really are") is the desire, from time to time, to impose your will on the world, calling such an imposition "justice" no doubt, as all empires (and protest movements) do, but draining that word of any objective correlate.

Of course, those who propagate today's left-wing neo-Gnosticism will say that they are implacably opposed, among other things, to the kind of "classic Christianity" represented by today's American right, including those responsible for current U.S. foreign policy. But here is the rub. The American religious right, though it has indeed got its finger on some elements of classic Christianity, is itself heavily compromised down very similar lines to what we might call the American religious left. The type of Christianity which has become popular in the last two centuries on both sides of the Atlantic, in fact, has steadily eroded its grip on the great New Testament and early Christian themes such as resurrection, and has embraced not only an individualism where what most truly matters is "my" soul, its state and its salvation, but also a future hope which is worryingly similar to that of Gnosticism. "Going to heaven when you die"—or, indeed, escaping death and going to heaven by means of a "rapture" instead—is the name of the game for millions of such Christians. And when you tell people, as I often do, that the New Testament isn't very interested in "going to heaven," but far more with a new bodily life at some future stage later on, and with the anticipation of that future bodily life in holiness and justice in the present, they look at you strangely, as if you were trying to inculcate a new heresy. "Conservative" post-Enlightenment Western Christianity and "liberal" post-Enlightenment Western Christianity begin to look as if they are simply the right and left wings of the same essentially wrongheaded movement.[2]

This is a theme for another time. I only raise it here to indicate the kind of larger map on which debates about documents such as the "Gospel of Judas" should be located. But we may note, as of particular interest, the response that might and perhaps should be made to the charge which the new Myth regularly levels against orthodox Christianity. The new Myth regularly charges orthodox Christianity with having negotiated a compromise with its surrounding culture, with having developed a theology that legitimates oppression, that won't offend people, that is really a power play in disguise. But this begins to look suspiciously like a case of what the psychoanalysts call "projection." If anyone has negotiated a cheerful compromise with the political status quo of the last two hundred years, it is precisely post-Enlightenment Western Protestantism, not least by agreeing that religion should be deemed a matter of private interest only, leaving the rest of life—the public square with all that it involves—to its own devices. As we saw, the classic Christians of the second and third centuries were indeed persecuted, while their gnostic contemporaries, by and large, were not. But modern Western Protestants are not persecuted. Why would they be? They are no danger to anyone with any power. Their Jesus is an escapist, not the Lord of the world. They pose no more challenge to the empires of today's world than the Gnostics did to Caesar. And my underlying point is that all this is so clear from a reading of "Judas" that it ought to make us sit up and think. Is that really what true Christian faith is all about?

The "Gospel of Judas," in fact, and the writings of those who have so enthusiastically commended it, ought to make us face up to some hard and important questions. Has "Judas" exposed the nonsense within the whole thing? Is it not clear that if we go with the new Myth and its version of neo-Gnosticism we are ultimately saying something about the meaning of the word "god" which ought to give us pause? Has the "Gospel of Judas" betrayed the dark secret of Gnosticism ancient and modern, that it believes that the god who made this world is a stupid, wicked sub-deity bent on mischief? And how many people, faced head on with that god on the one hand and the Father of Jesus Christ on the other—the latter being, by definition, the God who created the world out of pure self-giving love and has redeemed it by that same pure self-giving love, the God who reveals his glory in taking the weight of the world's evils on to his own shoulders in the person of his suffering son, the God who unveils his future plans for the created order in raising that son from the dead as the start of his new creation—how many people will seriously say that they don't much like the Christian God and prefer the gnostic one instead? If people really read and study the "Gospel of Judas," might we not predict that quite a number of them will conclude that Gnosticism is not, after all, for them?

Of course, Gnosticism ancient and modern holds out a baited hook. Accept its proposals, and you can find "divinity" within yourself. Your own deepest feelings and desires can be legitimized because, after all, if you have looked deeply within your own innermost being, what you have glimpsed is the self-authenticating spark of the divine. You don't, after all, need rescuing—except from the wicked world around you, not least the wicked world that has tried to squeeze you into its own shape, to make you just another duckling, and to mock you for your ugliness, when you knew all along that you were really a swan. Unlike the challenge of Jesus, this message doesn't tell you to deny yourself and take up your cross, but to discover yourself and follow your star. That is its great attraction. Unlike the promise of Jesus, however, this message doesn't offer you a world renewed and filled with the justice and joy of the God who made it, but a world rejected and scorned by those who have found a way of escaping it.

Classic Christianity, in short, has a lot more life and promise than have ever been imagined by those who propose the new Myth, or by those who offer newly discovered gnostic texts as the panacea for our ills. It is a shame that the churches have been so muzzled, so often self-blinded to the full dimensions of the gospel they profess, the gospel of Jesus himself. In that gospel, as opposed to that of "Judas," we discover a Jewish message intended for the whole world: a message about a creator God who loved the world so much he called the Jewish people to be the bearer of its salvation, and at the fullness of the times sent the Jewish Messiah to carry out that saving purpose; a message about this Messiah inaugurating the sovereign, wise, healing kingship of this creator God, in his actions and teaching and supremely and decisively in his death and resurrection; a message about the future completion of the new creation which began in the events concerning Jesus, a completion guaranteed by those events and to be put into operation by the power of the life-giving Spirit of this same creator God; a message which calls human beings of all sorts, not to discover a spark of divinity within, but to respond in gratitude and obedient faith to the powerful word which announces Jesus as the world's true Lord, and to discover in following him and belonging to his sacramentally constituted family a new dimension of life in the world rather than an invitation to escape from the world; a message which compels the followers of Jesus, energized by the power of his Spirit, to go out into the world and make new creation happen, confident that as that work has already begun in Jesus' resurrection, and will be completed when heaven and earth are united at last, so the signs of that completion can truly be brought to birth in changed lives and societies in the present time.

This is the real gospel. It has to do with the real Jesus, the real world, and above all the real God. As the advertisements say, accept no substitutes.

NOTES

In what follows, I have used the following abbreviations:

ANF   Ante-Nicene Fathers

GJud   "The Gospel of Judas"

KMW   *The Gospel of Judas,* edited by Rodolphe Kasser, Marvin Meyer and Gregor Wurst, with additional commentary by Bart D. Ehrman (Washington, DC: National Geographic, 2006).

Krosney   Herbert Krosney, *The Lost Gospel: The Quest for the Gospel of Judas Iscariot* (Washington, DC: National Geographic, 2006).

NHL   *The Nag Hammadi Library,* ed. James M. Robinson (Leiden: E. J. Brill, 1977).

NH 1, etc.   The Nag Hammadi codices themselves

Preface

1. On *The Da Vinci Code* (New York: Doubleday, 2003) see my short work, *Decoding Da Vinci* (Cambridge, England: Grove, 2006).

Chapter 1: Not Another New Gospel?

1. For details of these and other relevant data, see Bruce M. Metzger and Bart D. Ehrman, *The Text of the New Testament: Its Transmission, Corruption and Restoration*, 4th ed. (New York: Oxford University Press, 2005). For discussion, see various essays in B. D. Ehrman and M. W. Holmes eds., *The Text of the New Testament in Contemporary Research: Essays on the Status Quaestionis* (Grand Rapids, Mich.: Eerdmans, 1995).

2. J. M. Robinson, *The Secrets of Judas: The Story of the Misunderstood Disciple and His Lost Gospel* (San Francisco, Calif.: HarperSanFrancisco, 2006). Robinson's portrayal of Kasser amounts to burlesque (111, 160f.); and he constantly reminds us of his own distinguished status within the world of gnostic studies (e.g. 160, 186 n. 5).

3. The Letter of Peter to Philip is NH 8 (*NHL* 394–98).

4. The First Apocalypse of James is NH 5.3 (*NHL* 242–48).

5. "Allogenes" means "Stranger," one of the titles given in books of this type to Seth, the third son of Adam and Eve, who as we shall see is a key figure in the gnostic mythology in question.

6. An account of the carbon dating evidence can be found in Krosney, 269–74.

7. KMW, 34 n. 88 wrongly describes Irenaeus as Bishop of Lyon.

8. The quotation from Irenaeus is from *Against the Heresies*, 1.31.1.

9. The quotation is from Krosney, 275.

Chapter 2: Second-Century Gnosticism

1. The case against "Gnosticism" is made strongly by Michael A. Williams, *Rethinking "Gnosticism": An Argument for Dismantling a Dubious Category* (Princeton, NJ: Princeton University Press, 1996). See too Karen L. King, *What Is Gnosticism?* (Cambridge, Mass.: Belknap Press/Harvard University Press, 2003), and the somewhat strident statement of the point by Paul Mirecki in "Gnosis, Gnosticism," in *Eerdmans Dictionary of the Bible*, ed. D. N. Freedman (Grand Rapids, Mich.: Eerdmans, 2000), 508f.

2. Ehrman in KMW, 82–89; Meyer in KMW, 137–69.

3. References to Seth can be found in Gen. 4:25; 5:3.

4. KMW, 114.

5. Ehrman in KMW, 106.

6. On the Bar-Kochba revolt, see my *The New Testament and the People of God* (London and Minneapolis, Minn.: SPCK and Fortress Press, 1992), 164–66.

7. On continuing rabbinic affirmation of the creator God, see *The New Testament and the People of God*, 199f.

8. Paul's dismissal of "gnosis" can be found in 1 Corinthians 8:1. There are many similar hints elsewhere in 1 Corinthians.

9. 1 Timothy 6:20.

Chapter 3: The Judas of Faith and the Iscariot of History

1. Judah's birth is referred to in Genesis 29:35. The etymological derivation of the name was well enough known for Paul to make a pun on it even when writing in Greek (Romans 2:29).

2. The prophecy regarding the descent of the kings of Israel can be found in Micah 5:2.

3. For more on first-century Palestinian Jewish names, see Tal Ilan, *Lexicon of Jewish Names in Late Antiquity: Palestine 330 BCE–200 CE* (Texts and Studies in Ancient Judaism, 91) (Tübingen: Mohr Siebeck, 2002); Richard Bauckham, *Jesus and the Eyewitnesses: The Gospels as Eyewitness Testimony* (Grand Rapids, Mich.: Eerdmans [forthcoming in September 2006]).

4. See 1 Maccabees 2:1–5.

5. See Matthew 13:55; Mark 6:3; Jude 1.

6. Mark 3:13–19; Matthew 10:2–4; Luke 6:12–14; Acts 1:13. The last two put "Judas son of James" second to last; he may be the same person as "Thaddaeus" in Mark and Matthew. See my *Jesus and the Victory of God* (London and Minneapolis, Minn.: SPCK and Fortress, 1996), 300 n. 214.

7. Matthew 26:21–25; Mark 14:18–21; Luke 22:21–23; John 13:21–30.

8. On Judas's fondness of money, see John 12:6.

9. For the contrasting stories of Judas's death, see Matthew 27:3–10; Acts 1:18f.

10. For Satan's role in Judas's betrayal of Jesus, see Luke 22:3; John 13:2, 27.

11. George Steiner, *The Portage to San Cristobal of A.H.* (London: Faber, 1981).

12. See, e.g., Acts 2:23.

13. For modern explanations of Judas's behavior, see H. Maccoby, *Judas Iscariot and the Myth of Jewish Evil* (New York: Free Press, 1992); W. Klassen, *Judas: Betrayer or Friend of Jesus?* (Minneapolis, Minn.: Fortress, 1996).

14. Details of the early legends about Judas can be found in W. Klassen, "Judas Iscariot," in *Anchor Bible Dictionary*, ed. D. N. Freedman (New York: Doubleday, 1992), 3.1095. More instances in Robinson, *The Secrets of Judas*, chapter 3.

15. For references to Israel's god as "Saklas": GJud 51–53; see KMW, 37–39.

16. For the assertion that the Jesus of GJud has a sense of humor, see Meyer in KMW, 4; Kasser in KMW, 75f.

17. For Jesus mocking the disciples: Meyer in KMW, 4; see GJud 34 (KMW, 21); GJud 36f. (KMW, 24).

18. GJud 36f. (KMW, 24f.).

19. GJud 55 (KMW, 42).

20. E.g., Krosney, 278.

21. For the parallel in the Nag Hammadi texts, see Apoc. Pet. 81–83 (*NHL* 344).

22. NH 56.6–19.

23. Guy G. Stroumsa, in *Ha'Aretz*, April 1, 2006.

24. See the discussion in E. Pagels, *The Gnostic Gospels* (New York: Random House, 1976), 91f. (references are to the paperback edition: London: Phoenix Press, 2006).

25. GJud 56 (KMW, 45).

26. KMW, 43 n. 137; 96. Dr. John Dickson of Sydney, Australia, points out to me that the text does not (despite the assertion of the editors and commentators) have Jesus commanding Judas to hand him over. It could, that is, be merely a prediction. But it is a prediction with an evaluative comment: by handing him over, Judas will "exceed them all."

27. For Judas as "the thirteenth," see GJud 44, 46 (KMW, 31–33).

28. The extract is from GJud 57f. (KMW, 43f.). The ellipses at the end of the extract indicate considerable gaps in the text.

29. Krosney, 293.

30. Plato, *Timaeus*, 41d–42b. On "astral immortality," see my *The Resurrection of the Son of God* (London and Minneapolis, Minn.: SPCK and Fortress, 2003), 57–60, 110–12, 344–46.

31. Krosney, 299f.

32. Ehrman in KMW, 86, 105.

33. The extract is from GJud 49f. (KMW, 35f.).

34. Meyer's explanation can be found in KMW, 7f.

Chapter 4: When Is a Gospel Not a Gospel?

1. See Krosney, 135f., 155, 242, 245; and Robinson's own work, *The Secrets of Judas*, esp. 111, 130, 160f.

2. For details of Jesus in his historical context, see, e.g., my *Jesus and the Victory of God* (*Christian Origins and the Question of God*, vol. 2); *The Challenge of Jesus* (London and Downers Grove, Ill.: SPCK and IVP, 2000).

3. The extract is from Robinson, *The Secrets of Judas*, 75f.; emphasis original. Robinson goes on to make the same point about the "Gospel of Philip," the "Gospel of the Egyptians," and the "Gospel of Truth."

4. For the relationship between the gospels and ancient biography, see Richard J. Burridge, *What Are the Gospels? A Comparison with Graeco-Roman Biography* (Cambridge: Cambridge University Press, 1992).

5. Cf. Isaiah 40:9; 52:7.

6. The "Gospel of Peter" can be found in J. K. Elliott, ed., *The Apocryphal New Testament* (Oxford: Clarendon, 1993), 150–58. It is fair to point out that some of the second- and third-century orthodox writers declare that martyrs feel no pain.

7. For Jesus preaching to "those who are asleep," see "Gospel of Peter" 10:41f. (Elliott, 157). The theme seems related to 1 Peter 3:19f., which is itself notoriously hard to interpret.

8. The extract is from Ehrman in KMW, 102.

9. Meyer in KMW, 167.

10. This version of the "Temple" saying is from "Gospel of Thomas," saying 71.

11. Nobody, that is, until the "Gospel of Thomas," saying 53. On this whole point, see my *The New Testament and the People of God*, 421f.

12. For the Gospel of Judas's rejection of the emerging church, see GJud 38–43 (KMW, 25–29). Interestingly, none of

the first commentators on this document discusses its horror of sexual licence, including homosexual practice.

13. I have argued this at length in *The Resurrection of the Son of God*. I discuss the gnostic reinterpretation of "resurrection" in ch. 10. When Elaine Pagels cites the orthodox belief in Jesus' resurrection as a kind of odd extreme position (*The Gnostic Gospels*, 113), she shows that she has simply not understood how the early Christians thought.

14. For the dating of "Thomas," see esp. N. Perrin, *Thomas and Tatian: The Relationship Between the Gospel of Thomas and Tatian's Diatessaron* (Academia Biblica. Leiden/Atlanta, Ga.: Brill/Scholars Press, 2002).

15. See John 21:25; Acts 20:35.

16. For more detail on the dependence of the gnostic gospels upon the canonical gospels, cf. *Jesus and the Victory of God*, 230–39.

17. Pagels, quoted in Krosney, 278f.

18. Pagels, *The Gnostic Gospels*, 126f.

19. Ibid., 126.

Chapter 5: Lord of the World or Escaper from the World?

1. John 18:36. The key phrase is not to be translated "my kingdom is not *of* this world," as though Jesus meant that his kingship had nothing to do with this world. The Greek is *ek tou kosmou toutou*.

2. Matthew 28:18–20; Mark 13:10; 14:9; Luke 24:47; Acts 28:30f.; John 18:29–19:16; 20 and 21 *passim*.

3. *Paul: Fresh Perspectives* (in the USA, *Paul in Fresh Perspective*) (London and Minneapolis, Minn.: SPCK and Fortress, 2005), ch. 4.

4. Philippians 3:20f.

5. Revelation 21:2; 17:14; 19:16; Philippians 2:10.

6. See esp. Romans 8:18–27.

7. Cf. 1 Corinthians 15:20–28.

8. Martyrdom of Polycarp 9.3.

9. Martyrdom of Holy Martyrs, 4 (ANF 1.306).

10. Eusebius, *History of the Church* (*HE*) 5.1.1–5.2.8.

11. Irenaeus, *Against the Heresies* (*Adv. Haer.*) 5.1.63.

12. See Ephesians 3:10; Philippians 2:1–18.

13. For martyrdom as self-deception, see the discussion in Pagels, *The Gnostic Gospels*, 106f.

14. For the link between denial of Christ's suffering and rejection of martrydom, see Ignatius, *Epistle to the Trallians* 10.1; *Epistle to the Smyrneans* 5.1f. The point is clearly stated by Pagels, *The Gnostic Gospels*, 99.

15. For Justin's comments on his gnostic contemporaries, see his *Second Apology*, 15.

16. Eusebius's report on Basilides can be found in *HE* 4.7.7.

17. The extract is from Irenaeus, *Adv. Haer.* 1.24.6; see too 3.16.19–3.18.5.

18. Irenaeus, *Adv. Haer.* 3.18.5; 4.33.9.

19. Tertullian, *Scorpiace* 1.

20. The quote from Rowan Williams can be found in www.archbishopofcanterbury.org/sermons_speeches/060416a.htm. The point can be seen graphically in many NT texts, e.g., Hebrews 13:12–14.

21. The case is set out fully in *The Resurrection of the Son of God*.

22. The extract is from Ehrman in KMW, 84, 110 (emphasis original).

23. The extract is from Ehrman in KMW, 84.

24. John 8:32.

Chapter 6: Spinning Judas: The New Myth of Christian Origins

1. The extract is from Meyer in KMW, 9.

2. Meyer, 9–10.

3. Meyer, 10. He expands the point at 166–68, referring to other supposedly Christianized "Jewish gnostic" texts such as the "Secret Book of John" and "Eugnostos the Blessed."

4. A measured statement of the case for a "Jewish Gnosticism" can be found in, e.g., B. Pearson, *Gnosticism, Judaism and Egyptian Christianity* (Minneapolis, Minn.: Fortress, 1990).

5. Ehrman in Krosney, xxii, 51.

6. Ehrman, quoted in Krosney, 51.

7. For the gnostic rejection of the Jewish God, see Ehrman in KMW, 86. On "Thomas" see, e.g., saying 100: "Give to Caesar what belongs to Caesar, give to God what belongs to God—and

give to me what belongs to me" (in other words, Jesus represents a higher being than the "God" of the Jews).

8. Deuteronomy 6:4.

9. Guy G. Stroumsa, in *Ha'aretz*, April 1, 2006.

10. Amy-Jill Levine, "The Judas Gospel: Is It Good for the
Jews?", *The Jerusalem Report*, vol. 17.3 (May 2006), 46.

11. For Nussberger's view of her role, see *National Geographic*, May 2006, 95; Krosney, 169. She is later quoted as
saying that she was "guided by Providence" (Krosney, 175).

12. Krosney, 295. See too his conclusion (308), expressing
the hope that all this "will help to promote understanding of
those earlier times when Christianity diverged from its Judaic
origins, and that it will somehow bring not a sense of betrayal,
not a breaking of faith, but an increased sense of brotherhood
on this increasingly crowded planet." This text might indeed
enable fresh understanding of the first two centuries, but not
at all in the way Krosney imagines.

13. The extract is from Meyer in KMW, 166, 169. On this
"gospel" as "good news" see 45 n. 151.

14. The "new vistas" quote is from Ehrman in KMW, 80.

15. Against Krosney, 299.

16. See Krosney, 280.

17. The extract is from Krosney, 280, 286.

18. On the laughter of Jesus in the GJud see above, ch. 3
n. 16.

19. Galatians 2:20.

20. For more on the New Myth of Christian origins, see
my *Decoding Da Vinci*.

21. In support of the new Myth, see, e.g., B. Ehrman,
*Misquoting Jesus: The Story behind Who Changed the Bible and
Why* (San Francisco, Calif.: HarperSanFrancisco, 2005); *Lost
Christianities: The Battles for Scripture and the Faiths We Never Knew*
(New York: Oxford University Press, 2003); and several other
writings both scholarly and popular. As with various ancient
myths, these modern ones take on various shapes, and no one
writer should be taken as a straightforward embodiment of
the whole movement.

22. For the theory that the church sought power by speaking of a divine Jesus, see, e.g., Meyer in KMW, 7f., 27, 29,
118 ("in brief, one of the competing groups in Christianity
succeeded in overwhelming all the others"); Pagels, quoted

in Krosney, 191. The idea that the canonical gospels offer a "divine" Jesus whereas the gnostic texts offer a "human" one is one of the more bizarre, indeed demonstrably silly, proposals in Dan Brown's *The Da Vinci Code*.

23. Bagnall, quoted in Krosney, 196.

24. For parallels between Gnosticism and contemporary culture: Pagels, *The Gnostic Gospels*, e.g., 19, 27, 133, 140.

25. On Gnosticism and Feuerbach, see Pagels, 132.

26. Meyer, quoted in Krosney, 140.

27. Philip J. Lee, *Against the Protestant Gnostics* (New York: Oxford University Press, 1987). The 1993 paperback edition of the book contains a new preface noting the similarity of Lee's critique with that of the cultural commentator Harold Bloom, who has commented favorably on the work; Bloom's own book *The American Religion: The Emergence of the Post-Christian Nation* (New York: Touchstone, 1992) is a trenchant statement of a similar thesis.

28. C. O'Regan, *Gnostic Return in Modernity* (Albany, NY: State University of New York Press, 2001).

29. See above, ch. 5 n. 20.

30. For Lee on the sexual revolution, see *Against the Protestant Gnostics*, 197–205, quoting esp. Tom Wolfe, "The Me Decade and the Third Great Awakening," *Mauve Gloves and Madmen, Clutter and Vine* (New York: Bantam Books, 1977), 111–47. See too Lee, 277, on the contemporary "spiritualization of sexuality."

31. Pagels, *The Gnostic Gospels*, 149.

32. The "Left Behind" novels are the work of Tim F. LaHaye and Jerry B. Jenkins. The series of twelve books, published by Tyndale House Publishers, commenced in 1996 with *Left Behind: A Novel of the Earth's Last Days*.

33. On right-wing neo-Gnosticism, see esp. Lee, 168–72, 244f., 268.

34. See again Lee, 277, speaking of a "spiritualization of sexuality."

35. The extract is from Krosney, 300.

Chapter 7: The Challenge of "Judas" for Today

1. See, e.g., Ephesians 1:10; Revelation 21–22.

2. On the roots of this, see Lee, ch. 6.

N. T. Wright is Bishop of Durham. He is one of the world's foremost New Testament scholars, a regular broadcaster and bestselling author. Several of his books have won awards, including *The Resurrection of the Son of God* (one of three volumes in his magisterial Christian Origins and the Question of God series) and a number of titles from his popular For Everyone series of New Testament guides. Dr. Wright is a member of the International Anglican Doctrinal and Theological Commission, and was also part of the Lambeth Commission that wrote *The Windsor Report.*

The seven photos found
in this book are of the
Gospel of Judas contained
in Codex Tchacos and were
taken by photographer
Kenneth Garrett.